THE

FSG POETRY

ANTHOLOGY

THE

FSG POETRY

ANTHOLOGY

Edited by

JONATHAN GALASSI

and ROBYN CRESWELL

Farrar, Straus and Giroux   New York

Farrar, Straus and Giroux
120 Broadway, New York 10271

Owing to limitations of space, a list of sources and of permissions
to reprint the poems can be found on pages 383–396.

The Library of Congress has cataloged the hardcover edition as follows:
Names: Galassi, Jonathan, editor. | Creswell, Robyn, editor. | Farrar, Straus, and Giroux.
Title: The FSG Poetry Anthology / edited by Jonathan Galassi and Robyn Creswell.
Other titles: Farrar, Straus and Giroux poetry anthology
Description: First edition. | New York : Farrar, Straus and Giroux, 2021. | Includes index.
Identifiers: LCCN 2021025314 | ISBN 9780374159115 (hardcover)
Subjects: LCSH: Poetry—Collections. | Poetry—Translations into English. | LCGFT: Poetry
Classification: LCC PN6101 .F74 2021 | DDC 808.81—dc23
LC record available at https://lccn.loc.gov/2021025314

Paperback ISBN: 9780374606442

Designed by Gretchen Achilles

Our books may be purchased in bulk for promotional, educational,
or business use. Please contact your local bookseller or the Macmillan Corporate
and Premium Sales Department at 1-800-221-7945, extension 5442,
or by email at MacmillanSpecialMarkets@macmillan.com.

www.fsgbooks.com
www.twitter.com/fsgbooks • www.facebook.com/fsgbooks

1   3   5   7   9   10   8   6   4   2

In Memory of Robert Giroux

Contents

Introduction   xv

BEGINNINGS: 1950s–1970s

THE 1980s AND 1990s

THE 2000s

THE 2010s

THE 2020s

Introduction

Farrar and Straus, the last of the small independent houses of its kind, was founded by Roger Straus and John Farrar in 1946. They bumped along, publishing whatever they could get their hands on with the collaboration of a number of other partners, until 1955, when Robert Giroux joined the firm, which was known by then as Farrar, Straus and Cudahy. Giroux had had a distinguished career as a literary editor at Harcourt, Brace and Company, one of the leading publishers of the prewar era, but he'd fallen out with new management and suddenly found himself "on the beach," as his new boss, who had known Bob in the navy during the war, liked to put it. Roger soon made Bob his editor in chief, and a string of leading writers—among them John Berryman, Jack Kerouac, Robert Lowell, Flannery O'Connor, and Jean Stafford—eventually followed him, resetting the tone and direction of the list once and for all. Bob's arrival was, as Roger noted, "the single most important thing to happen to this company." In 1964 it became Farrar, Straus and Giroux in recognition of his decisive contribution.[*]

As the list above indicates, several of Giroux's signal writers were poets, and from the moment he arrived poetry assumed a place at the heart of the company's identity. Berryman, his closest friend at Columbia College, was a lifelong comrade, and his groundbreaking poem *Homage to Mistress Bradstreet* became the first book Giroux published at his new home, in 1956. *Homage* laid the foundation for a generation of FSG poets, which would include not only Lowell and his friend Elizabeth Bishop but also Randall Jarrell, Allen Tate, and Louise Bogan.[†] The house also published a number of prominent poets in translation—Juan Ramón Jiménez, Pablo Neruda, Salvatore Quasimodo, and Nelly Sachs, all recipients of the Nobel Prize in Literature—and this internationalist leaning was likewise a sign of things to come.

---

[*] *Hothouse: The Art of Survival and the Survival of Art at America's Most Celebrated Publishing House, Farrar, Straus and Giroux* (2013), by Boris Kachka, tells much of the story, often accurately.

[†] See Eileen Simpson's *Poets in their Youth* (1982) for an affecting portrait of the early triumphs and trials of Berryman, Lowell, Giroux, and their friends.

Another relationship that would have major consequences for FSG was Giroux's friendship with T. S. Eliot, not only the most renowned poet of the century (he too had received the Nobel Prize, in 1948) but also the motivating editorial spirit at Faber and Faber, the London publisher he had helped build into one of the English-speaking world's most influential. Thanks to Eliot, the Faber list, which featured not only Eliot himself but also Ezra Pound, Marianne Moore, and W. H. Auden, had unquestioned poetic primacy in Britain.* The partnership forged by Giroux and Eliot, who also published his last books at Giroux's new house, continued to thrive under Charles Monteith, Eliot's successor as Faber's literary editor, who brought on Philip Larkin, Thom Gunn, Seamus Heaney, and Ted Hughes—all eventually also published by FSG. This cross-fertilization proved especially fruitful, since a number of later Faber poets, from Heaney to Michael Hofmann, were strongly affected by Lowell, while others, including Derek Walcott, joined Faber via FSG. Though the two houses have very different lists and identities, they share the conviction that poetry is fundamental to literary expression, that it is here the writer strikes their distinctive note most powerfully.

To mark FSG's seventy-fifth anniversary, we have assembled an anthology—in all honesty, never one of Roger's favorite kinds of books—in honor of Bob Giroux's signal contribution to our DNA, and to underline poetry's continued centrality to the house. It includes work by nearly all the poets published here since Bob's arrival, presented in broadly chronological sections. This affords some sense of how the company's editorial perspectives have evolved over the decades, and how the scope of FSG's poetry has gradually expanded from Giroux's classic core in widening, more or less concentric circles. The poems are designated by the date of their first publication on the FSG list, which occasionally makes for unexpected juxtapositions. Certain poets one might have expected to find among the house's early offerings have only recently arrived: Marianne Moore, for instance, finally showed up in 2017, in Heather Cass White's new edition. Echoes of the incisive intricacies of Moore's verse, though, can be heard in the work of younger poets as different as Maureen N. McLane, Ange Mlinko, and Carl Phillips.

FSG poetry has never been a school so much as a congeries of individual

---

* Toby Faber's *Faber & Faber: The Untold Story* (2019), drawn largely from the Faber files, shows how Geoffrey Faber, Eliot, Charles Monteith, and others built their house.

sensibilities; still, in the modernist schism marked by the Eliot-Pound divergence, the house fell squarely on Eliot's side of the line, while James Laughlin at New Directions championed the objectivists and their heirs, the Black Mountain poets. FSG mainly eschewed the Beats, despite Giroux's friendship with Jack Kerouac, and much of the New York School—a missed opportunity. Nevertheless, during the seventies, eighties, and nineties, we welcomed poets as diverse as James Wright and James Schuyler, Gjertrud Schnackenberg, Joseph Brodsky, Frederick Seidel, John Ashbery, Frank Bidart, Adam Zagajewski, and Les Murray. They joined a list of equally distinct prose writers who were helping to shape American letters, among them Joan Didion, Susan Sontag, Philip Roth, Grace Paley, John McPhee, Jamaica Kincaid, Lydia Davis, Tom Wolfe, and many, many others.

The poetry of the last two decades has embraced the multifariousness of the culture and the competing (if often complementary) interests of innovation and tradition. One satisfaction in selecting and arranging this anthology has been to see how contemporary poets have harmonized, wittingly or not, with their precursors, creating a sort of living choir, however diffused across space and time. In some poems, such as Christopher Logue's cinematic rewriting of Homer, the juxtaposition of old and new is the whole point, while Louise Glück's reinhabiting of classical myth makes it urgently our own. But we hadn't anticipated the echoes, for example, between Aleksandr Solzhenitsyn's evocation of the looting of German cities at the close of World War II (in his long poem "Prussian Nights"), Durs Grünbein's "Lament of a Legionnaire," on Roman campaigns in Germania, and Mahmoud Darwish's elegy for the Moorish cities of Andalusia after the Reconquista ("On the Last Evening on this Earth"). We hope that some of the pleasure we had in discovering these unexpected harmonies will resonate in the reader as well.

The book closes with the poets of the 2020s, recently or soon to be published, and features work by writers from Belarus, Egypt, Jamaica, and elsewhere. There are new recuperations too, including Lowell's old friend and sparring partner Delmore Schwartz (also the subject of a moving Berryman elegy, included here), and the founder of modern poetry himself, Charles Baudelaire.

We have aimed to single out poems that come alive as objects on their own, even as they rhyme—often at a slant—with other pieces in the anthology. There are greatest hits here, but more frequently we've tried to select work that is perhaps less familiar yet nevertheless characteristic of the writer: renewed discoveries to hold up to the light again.

Above all, we hope this book is fun—full of surprises and delights that will lead the reader back to the wealth of extraordinary voices who have helped make FSG the house it is.

ROBYN CRESWELL AND JONATHAN GALASSI

BEGINNINGS
1950s–1970s

Dream Song #22

Of 1826

I am the little man who smokes & smokes.
I am the girl who does know better but.
I am the king of the pool.
I am so wise I had my mouth sewn shut.
I am a government official & a goddamned fool.
I am a lady who takes jokes.

I am the enemy of the mind.
I am the auto salesman and lóve you.
I am a teenage cancer, with a plan.
I am the blackt-out man.
I am the woman powerful as a zoo.
I am two eyes screwed to my set, whose blind—

It is the Fourth of July.
Collect: while the dying man,
forgone by you creator, who forgives,
is gasping "Thomas Jefferson still lives"
in vain, in vain, in vain.
I am Henry Pussy-cat! My whiskers fly.

1964

We Are Many

Of the many men who I am, who we are,
I can't find a single one;
they disappear among my clothes,
they've left for another city.

When everything seems to be set
to show me off as intelligent,
the fool I always keep hidden
takes over all that I say.

At other times, I'm asleep
among distinguished people,
and when I look for my brave self,
a coward unknown to me
rushes to cover my skeleton
with a thousand fine excuses.

When a decent house catches fire,
instead of the fireman I summon,
an arsonist bursts on the scene,
and that's me. What can I do?
What can I do to distinguish myself?
How can I pull myself together?

All the books I read
are full of dazzling heroes,
always sure of themselves.
I die with envy of them;
and in films full of wind and bullets,
I goggle at the cowboys,
I even admire the horses.

But when I call for a hero,
out comes my lazy old self;
so I never know who I am,
nor how many I am or will be.
I'd love to be able to touch a bell
and summon the real me,
because if I really need myself,
I mustn't disappear.

While I am writing, I'm far away;
and when I come back, I've gone.
I would like to know if others
go through the same things that I do,
have as many selves as I have,
and see themselves similarly;
and when I've exhausted this problem,
I'm going to study so hard
that when I explain myself,
I'll be talking geography.

1974

Translated by Alastair Reid

A Dedication to my Wife

To whom I owe the leaping delight
That quickens my senses in our wakingtime
And the rhythm that governs the repose of our sleepingtime,
    The breathing in unison

Of lovers whose bodies smell of each other
Who think the same thoughts without need of speech
And babble the same speech without need of meaning.

No peevish winter wind shall chill
No sullen tropic sun shall wither
The roses in the rose-garden which is ours and ours only

But this dedication is for others to read:
These are private words addressed to you in public.

This is a 1963 revision of Eliot's dedication to *The Elder Statesman*, which was published by
FSG in 1959.

ROBERT LOWELL

Skunk Hour

(For Elizabeth Bishop)

Nautilus Island's hermit
heiress still lives through winter in her Spartan cottage;
her sheep still graze above the sea.
Her son's a bishop. Her farmer
is first selectman in our village;
she's in her dotage.

Thirsting for
the hierarchic privacy
of Queen Victoria's century,
she buys up all
the eyesores facing her shore,
and lets them fall.

The season's ill—
we've lost our summer millionaire,
who seemed to leap from an L. L. Bean
catalogue. His nine-knot yawl
was auctioned off to lobstermen.
A red fox stain covers Blue Hill.

And now our fairy
decorator brightens his shop for fall;
his fishnet's filled with orange cork,
orange, his cobbler's bench and awl;
there is no money in his work,
he'd rather marry.

One dark night,
my Tudor Ford climbed the hill's skull;
I watched for love-cars. Lights turned down,
they lay together, hull to hull,
where the graveyard shelves on the town. . . .
My mind's not right.

A car radio bleats,
"Love, O careless Love. . . ." I hear
my ill-spirit sob in each blood cell,
as if my hand were at its throat. . . .
I myself am hell;
nobody's here—

only skunks, that search
in the moonlight for a bite to eat.
They march on their soles up Main Street:
white stripes, moonstruck eyes' red fire
under the chalk-dry and spar spire
of the Trinitarian Church.

I stand on top
of our back steps and breathe the rich air—
a mother skunk with her column of kittens swills the garbage pail.
She jabs her wedge-head in a cup
of sour cream, drops her ostrich tail,
and will not scare.

1959

Cape Breton

Out on the high "bird islands," Ciboux and Hertford,
the razorbill auks and the silly-looking puffins all stand
with their backs to the mainland
in solemn, uneven lines along the cliff's brown grass-frayed edge,
while the few sheep pastured there go "Baaa, baaa."
(Sometimes, frightened by aeroplanes, they stampede
and fall over into the sea or onto the rocks.)
The silken water is weaving and weaving,
disappearing under the mist equally in all directions,
lifted and penetrated now and then
by one shag's dripping serpent-neck,
and somewhere the mist incorporates the pulse,
rapid but unurgent, of a motorboat.

The same mist hangs in thin layers
among the valleys and gorges of the mainland
like rotting snow-ice sucked away
almost to spirit; the ghosts of glaciers drift
among those folds and folds of fir: spruce and hackmatack—
dull, dead, deep peacock-colors,
each riser distinguished from the next
by an irregular nervous saw-tooth edge,
alike, but certain as a stereoscopic view.

The wild road clambers along the brink of the coast.
On it stand occasional small yellow bulldozers,
but without their drivers, because today is Sunday.
The little white churches have been dropped into the matted hills
like lost quartz arrowheads.
The road appears to have been abandoned.

Whatever the landscape had of meaning appears to have been abandoned,
unless the road is holding it back, in the interior,
where we cannot see,
where deep lakes are reputed to be,
and disused trails and mountains of rock
and miles of burnt forests standing in gray scratches
like the admirable scriptures made on stones by stones—
and these regions now have little to say for themselves
except in thousands of light song-sparrow songs floating upward
freely, dispassionately, through the mist, and meshing
in brown-wet, fine, torn fish-nets.

A small bus comes along, in up-and-down rushes,
packed with people, even to its step.
(On weekdays with groceries, spare automobile parts, and pump parts,
but today only two preachers extra, one carrying his frock coat on a hanger.)
It passes the closed roadside stand, the closed schoolhouse,
where today no flag is flying
from the rough-adzed pole topped with a white china doorknob.
It stops, and a man carrying a baby gets off,
climbs over a stile, and goes down through a small steep meadow,
which establishes its poverty in a snowfall of daisies,
to his invisible house beside the water.

The birds keep on singing, a calf bawls, the bus starts.
The thin mist follows
the white mutations of its dream;
an ancient chill is rippling the dark brooks.

1969

Next Day

Moving from Cheer to Joy, from Joy to All,
I take a box
And add it to my wild rice, my Cornish game hens.
The slacked or shorted, basketed, identical
Food-gathering flocks
Are selves I overlook. Wisdom, said William James,

Is learning what to overlook. And I am wise
If that is wisdom.
Yet somehow, as I buy All from these shelves
And the boy takes it to my station wagon,
What I've become
Troubles me even if I shut my eyes.

When I was young and miserable and pretty
And poor, I'd wish
What all girls wish: to have a husband,
A house and children. Now that I'm old, my wish
Is womanish:
That the boy putting groceries in my car

See me. It bewilders me he doesn't see me.
For so many years
I was good enough to eat: the world looked at me
And its mouth watered. How often they have undressed me,
The eyes of strangers!
And, holding their flesh within my flesh, their vile

Imaginings within my imagining,
I too have taken
The chance of life. Now the boy pats my dog
And we start home. Now I am good.
The last mistaken,
Ecstatic, accidental bliss, the blind

Happiness that, bursting, leaves upon the palm
Some soap and water—
It was so long ago, back in some Gay
Twenties, Nineties, I don't know . . . Today I miss
My lovely daughter
Away at school, my sons away at school,

My husband away at work—I wish for them.
The dog, the maid,
And I go through the sure unvarying days
At home in them. As I look at my life,
I am afraid
Only that it will change, as I am changing:

I am afraid, this morning, of my face.
It looks at me
From the rear-view mirror, with the eyes I hate,
The smile I hate. Its plain, lined look
Of gray discovery
Repeats to me: "You're old." That's all, I'm old.

And yet I'm afraid, as I was at the funeral
I went to yesterday.
My friend's cold made-up face, granite among its flowers,
Her undressed, operated-on, dressed body
Were my face and body.
As I think of her I hear her telling me

How young I seem; I *am* exceptional;
I think of all I have.
But really no one is exceptional,
No one has anything, I'm anybody,
I stand beside my grave
Confused with my life, that is commonplace and solitary.

1969

from "Seasons of the Soul"

Autumn

It had an autumn smell
And that was how I knew
That I was down a well:
I was no longer young;
My lips were numb and blue,
The air was like fine sand
In a butcher's stall
Or pumice to the tongue:
And when I raised my hand
I stood in the empty hall.

The round ceiling was high
And the gray light like shale
Thin, crumbling, and dry:
No rug on the bare floor
Nor any carved detail
To which the eye could glide;
I counted along the wall
Door after closed door
Through which a shade might slide
To the cold and empty hall.

I will leave this house, I said,
There is the autumn weather—
Here, nor living nor dead;
The lights burn in the town
Where men fear together.

Then on the bare floor,
But tiptoe lest I fall,
I walked years down
Towards the front door
At the end of the empty hall.

The door was false—no key
Or lock, and I was caught
In the house; yet I could see
I had been born to it
For miles of running brought
Me back where I began.
I saw now in the wall
A door open a slit
And a fat grizzled man
Come out into the hall:

As in a moonlit street
Men meeting are too shy
To check their hurried feet
But raise their eyes and squint
As through a needle's eye
Into the faceless gloom,—
My father in a gray shawl
Gave me an unseeing glint
And entered another room!
I stood in the empty hall

And watched them come and go
From one room to another,
Old men, old women—slow,
Familiar; girls, boys;
I saw my downcast mother
Clad in her street-clothes,
Her blue eyes long and small,

Who had no look or voice
For him whose vision froze
Him in the empty hall.

1977

Long Live Spring

New York, the virago with dirty nails, wakes up. As the clear stars at nightfall come surging into the light from darkness, so do the black ships in the turbid Hudson, anchored in an iron circle. Day is taking its place and picks up the telephone in its Broadway office.

Springtime comes, with a desire for purity reinforced by the dawn, swimming through the sky and water to the city. All night she has been awake beautifying herself, bathing in the light of the full moon. For a moment her roses, still warm, reflect the beauty of the dawn which is struggling with the trust, "Smoke, Shadow, Mud and Co.," which receives her with its pilot. But alas the dawn falls back into the water almost defeated. Armies of gold come in the sun to aid her. They draw her out dripping and naked and give her artificial respiration in the Statue of Liberty. The poor thing! How delighted she is, still timid though conquering!

The pale gold of nine o'clock is enough to make her a queen. Yes, the dirty buds on the trees on the piers smile with a blond grace; the sparrows on the fire escapes sing matters of gold, still black with memories of snow, the cemeteries on the shores explode the soot into thin sparks, a pink band in the east enchants the signs on the towers, bells of fire alarms and all the church bells ring in confusion . . .

Behold her! She is here now, naked and strong in Washington Square, beneath the arch, ready to march up Fifth Avenue toward the park, her naked thighs already begin to mark time, without moving forward. She bends her head. Now!

Long live spring! Long live spring! Long live spring!

1957

Translated by H. R. Hays

LOUISE BOGAN

Night

The cold remote islands
And the blue estuaries
Where what breathes, breathes
The restless wind of the inlets,
And what drinks, drinks
The incoming tide;

Where shell and weed
Wait upon the salt wash of the sea,
And the clear nights of stars
Swing their lights westward
To set behind the land;

Where the pulse clinging to the rocks
Renews itself forever;
Where, again on cloudless nights,
The water reflects
The firmament's partial setting;

—O remember
In your narrowing dark hours
That more things move
Than blood in the heart.

1968

NELLY SACHS

"When sleep enters the body like smoke"

When sleep enters the body like smoke
and man journeys into the abyss
like an extinguished star that is lighted elsewhere,
then all quarrel ceases,
overworked nag that has tossed the nightmare grip
of its rider.
Released from their secret rhythm
are the steps
that knock like well lifts at the earth's enigma.
All artificial deaths have returned to the bloody confusion
of their nests.

When sleep enters the body like smoke
the stilled child breathes with the moon trumpet in its arm.
The tear oversleeps its longing to flow,
but love has completed all detours
and rests in its beginning.
Now is the time for the calf to test
its new tongue on its mother's body,
the wrong key does not lock
and the knife rusts far
into the pale heath of dawn
which blossoms out of the oblivion
with the early morning's fearful red.

When sleep leaves the body like smoke
and man, sated with secrets,
drives the overworked nag of quarrel
out of its stall,
then the fire-breathing union begins anew

and death wakens in every bud of May
and the child kisses a stone
in the eclipse of the stars.

1967

Translated by Michael Roloff

O My Sweet Animals

Now autumn spoils the green of hills,
o my sweet animals. Again we'll hear,
before night falls, the last lament
of birds, the call of the gray plain
that goes to meet that high sound
of the sea. And the smell of wood
in the rain, the smell of dens,
how it lives here among the houses,
among the men, o my sweet animals.
This face that turns its slow eyes,
this hand that points to the sky
where thunder drones, are yours, my wolves,
o my foxes burnt by blood.
Each hand, each face, is yours.
You, love, tell me all was vain:
life, the days corroded by a water
assiduous, while from the gardens
rises a children's song. Are they distant,
then, from us? But they yield in the air,
barely shadows. This your voice.
But I perhaps do know all has not been.

1960

Translated by Allen Mandelbaum

Dream Song #29

There sat down, once, a thing on Henry's heart
só heavy, if he had a hundred years
& more, & weeping, sleepless, in all them time
Henry could not make good.
Starts again always in Henry's ears
the little cough somewhere, an odour, a chime.

And there is another thing he has in mind
like a grave Sienese face a thousand years
would fail to blur the still profiled reproach of. Ghastly,
with open eyes, he attends, blind.
All the bells say: too late. This is not for tears;
thinking.

But never did Henry, as he thought he did,
end anyone and hacks her body up
and hide the pieces, where they may be found.
He knows: he went over everyone, & nobody's missing.
Often he reckons, in the dawn, them up.
Nobody is ever missing.

1964

Losses

It was not dying: everybody died.
It was not dying: we had died before
In the routine crashes—and our fields
Called up the papers, wrote home to our folks,
And the rates rose, all because of us.
We died on the wrong page of the almanac,
Scattered on mountains fifty miles away;
Diving on haystacks, fighting with a friend,
We blazed up on the lines we never saw.
We died like aunts or pets or foreigners.
(When we left high school nothing else had died
For us to figure we had died like.)

In our new planes, with our new crews, we bombed
The ranges by the desert or the shore,
Fired at towed targets, waited for our scores—
And turned into replacements and woke up
One morning, over England, operational.
It wasn't different: but if we died
It was not an accident but a mistake
(But an easy one for anyone to make).
We read our mail and counted up our missions—
In bombers named for girls, we burned
The cities we had learned about in school—
Till our lives wore out; our bodies lay among
The people we had killed and never seen.
When we lasted long enough they gave us medals;
When we died they said, "Our casualties were low."
They said, "Here are the maps"; we burned the cities.

It was not dying—no, not ever dying;
But the night I died I dreamed that I was dead,
And the cities said to me: "Why are you dying?
We are satisfied, if you are; but why did I die?"

1969

from *Prussian Nights*

"In Neidenburg conflagrations shiver"

In Neidenburg conflagrations shiver
To shards old masonry's good stone.
The town's a chaos; in a fever
Of acquisition our pursuit
Takes it, then throws it aside for one
More wave of our soldiery to share.
No Germans here in uniform
Or civvies now. But in the warm
Walls their comforts wait our care—
And through the fires, the smoke, the soot,
The Conquerors of Europe swarm,
Russians scurrying everywhere.
In their trucks they stuff the loot:
Vacuum cleaners, wine and candles,
Skirts and picture frames and pipes,
Brooches, medallions, blouses, buckles,
Typewriters (not with Russian type),
Rings of sausages, and cheeses,
Small domestic ware and veils,
Combs and forks and wineglasses,
Samplers, and shoes, and scales . . .
While on the tower of the town hall,
Through a rent in the smoky sky,
The clock, surviving through it all,
Measures the time as honorably
Between the others and ourselves,
Those who've come and those who've fled,

With the same ever-even tread,
Only the ancient hands' fine lace
Is trembling slightly on its face.

1977

Translated by Robert Conquest

Pilgrims

For S & R.F

Standing there they began to grow skins
dappled as trees, alone in the flare
of their own selves: the fire
died down in the open ground

and they made a place for themselves.
It wasn't much good,
they'd fall, and freeze,

some of them said
Well, it was all they could,

some said it was beautiful, some days,
the way the little ones took to the water,
and some lay smoking, smoking,

and some burned up for good,
and some waited,
lasting, staring
over each other's merciful shoulders,
listening:
        only high in a sudden January thaw
or safe a second in some unsmiling eyes
they'd known always

whispering
Why are we in this life.

1969

Waking Early Sunday Morning

O to break loose, like the chinook
salmon jumping and falling back,
nosing up to the impossible
stone and bone-crushing waterfall—
raw-jawed, weak-fleshed there, stopped by ten
steps of the roaring ladder, and then
to clear the top on the last try,
alive enough to spawn and die.

Stop, back off. The salmon breaks
water, and now my body wakes
to feel the unpolluted joy
and criminal leisure of a boy—
no rainbow smashing a dry fly
in the white run is free as I,
here squatting like a dragon on
time's hoard before the day's begun!

Vermin run for their unstopped holes;
in some dark nook a fieldmouse rolls
a marble, hours on end, then stops;
the termite in the woodwork sleeps—
listen, the creatures of the night
obsessive, casual, sure of foot,
go on grinding, while the sun's
daily remorseful blackout dawns.

Fierce, fireless mind, running downhill.
Look up and see the harbor fill:
business as usual in eclipse

goes down to the sea in ships—
wake of refuse, dacron rope,
bound for Bermuda or Good Hope,
all bright before the morning watch
the wine-dark hulls of yawl and ketch.

I watch a glass of water wet
with a fine fuzz of icy sweat,
silvery colors touched with sky,
serene in their neutrality—
yet if I shift, or change my mood,
I see some object made of wood,
background behind it of brown grain,
to darken it, but not to stain.

O that the spirit could remain
tinged but untarnished by its strain!
Better dressed and stacking birch,
or lost with the Faithful at Church—
anywhere, but somewhere else!
And now the new electric bells,
clearly chiming, "Faith of our fathers,"
and now the congregation gathers.

O Bible chopped and crucified
in hymns we hear but do not read,
none of the milder subtleties
of grace or art will sweeten these
stiff quatrains shovelled out four-square—
they sing of peace, and preach despair;
yet they gave darkness some control,
and left a loophole for the soul.

No, put old clothes on, and explore
the corners of the woodshed for
its dregs and dreck: tools with no handle,

ten candle-ends not worth a candle,
old lumber banished from the Temple,
damned by Paul's precept and example,
cast from the kingdom, banned in Israel,
the wordless sign, the tinkling cymbal.

When will we see Him face to face?
Each day, He shines through darker glass.
In this small town where everything
is known, I see His vanishing
emblems, His white spire and flag-
pole sticking out above the fog,
like old white china doorknobs, sad,
slight, useless things to calm the mad.

Hammering military splendor,
top-heavy Goliath in full armor—
little redemption in the mass
liquidations of their brass,
elephant and phalanx moving
with the times and still improving,
when that kingdom hit the crash:
a million foreskins stacked like trash . . .

Sing softer! But what if a new
diminuendo brings no true
tenderness, only restlessness,
excess, the hunger for success,
sanity or self-deception
fixed and kicked by reckless caution,
while we listen to the bells—
anywhere, but somewhere else!

O to break loose. All life's grandeur
is something with a girl in summer . . .
elated as the President
girdled by his establishment
this Sunday morning, free to chaff
his own thoughts with his bear-cuffed staff,
swimming nude, unbuttoned, sick
of his ghost-written rhetoric!

No weekends for the gods now. Wars
flicker, earth licks its open sores,
fresh breakage, fresh promotions, chance
assassinations, no advance.
Only man thinning out his kind
sounds through the Sabbath noon, the blind
swipe of the pruner and his knife
busy about the tree of life . . .

Pity the planet, all joy gone
from this sweet volcanic cone;
peace to our children when they fall
in small war on the heels of small
war—until the end of time
to police the earth, a ghost
orbiting forever lost
in our monotonous sublime.

1967

The First Days

Optima dies prima fugit

The first thing I saw in the morning
Was a huge golden bee ploughing
His burly right shoulder into the belly
Of a sleek yellow pear
Low on a bough.
Before he could find that sudden black honey
That squirms around in there
Inside the seed, the tree could not bear any more.
The pear fell to the ground,
With the bee still half alive
Inside its body.
He would have died if I hadn't knelt down
And sliced the pear gently
A little more open.
The bee shuddered, and returned.
Maybe I should have left him alone there,
Drowning in his own delight.
The best days are the first
To flee, sang the lovely
Musician born in this town
So like my own.
I let the bee go
Among the gasworks at the edge of Mantua.

1977

Ravenna (1)

I, too, have been in Ravenna.
It is a little dead city
That has churches and a good many ruins.
You can read about it in books.

You walk back through it and look around you:
The streets are so muddy and damp, and so
Dumbstruck for a thousand years,
And moss and grass, everywhere.

That is what old songs are like—
You listen to them, and nobody laughs
And everybody draws back into
His own time till night falls into him.

1970

Translated by James Wright

The Road to Tucumcari

The road to Tucumcari
is the mulch of bones
and intonation
leading westward.

Trucks throw rods in midwinter,
there's no place to sleep,
no money, or it's too late
Near the New Mexico border.

And you wake up shaking,
a shaking face wakes you saying,
in the frosted light, can you take me
to Tucumcari, truck's thrown a rod.

You are no longer
on the road to California.
You're eating breakfast
with a native of Floyd County, Texas.

And the deer and the ducks and the rabbits
was numerous and is
says the tobacco stain
that runs from chin to navel.

A hand so hard and cold
had to earn its first dollar
hauling frozen cattle
off the roads.

Cold car. Cold talk. Worst weather seen.
Blizzard of nineteen-seventeen.
His brother's mule!
Hand held in mine!

What's left to uncover
under the battered U-roll-it
but the half a head he lost last year
falling out of the pickup.

Toward noon,
under sun, beside juniper,
I too can pronounce Tucumcari,
Anywhere, forever.

1969

DEREK WALCOTT

Sea Grapes

That sail which leans on light,
tired of islands,
a schooner beating up the Caribbean

for home, could be Odysseus,
home-bound on the Aegean;
that father and husband's

longing, under gnarled sour grapes, is
like the adulterer hearing Nausicaa's name
in every gull's outcry.

This brings nobody peace. The ancient war
between obsession and responsibility
will never finish and has been the same

for the sea-wanderer or the one on shore
now wriggling on his sandals to walk home,
since Troy sighed its last flame,

and the blind giant's boulder heaved the trough
from whose groundswell the great hexameters come
to the conclusions of exhausted surf.

The classics can console. But not enough.

1976

PHILIP LARKIN

Sad Steps

Groping back to bed after a piss
I part thick curtains, and am startled by
The rapid clouds, the moon's cleanliness.

Four o'clock: wedge-shadowed gardens lie
Under a cavernous, a wind-picked sky.
There's something laughable about this,

The way the moon dashes through clouds that blow
Loosely as cannon-smoke to stand apart
(Stone-coloured light sharpening the roofs below)

High and preposterous and separate—
Lozenge of love! Medallion of art!
O wolves of memory! Immensements! No,

One shivers slightly, looking up there.
The hardness and the brightness and the plain
Far-reaching singleness of that wide stare

Is a reminder of the strength and pain
Of being young; that it can't come again,
But is for others undiminished somewhere.

1974

Rites of Passage

Something is taking place.
Horns bud bright in my hair.
My feet are turning hoof.
And Father, see my face
—Skin that was damp and fair
Is barklike and, feel, rough.

See Greytop how I shine.
I rear, break loose, I neigh
Snuffing the air, and harden
Toward a completion, mine.
And next I make my way
Adventuring through your garden.

My play is earnest now.
I canter to and fro.
My blood, it is like light.
Behind an almond bough,
Horns gaudy with its snow,
I wait live, out of sight.

All planned before my birth
For you, Old Man, no other,
Whom your groin's trembling warns.
I stamp upon the earth
A message to my mother.
And then I lower my horns.

1973

SEAMUS HEANEY

Oysters

Our shells clacked on the plates.
My tongue was a filling estuary,
My palate hung with starlight:
As I tasted the salty Pleiades
Orion dipped his foot into the water.

Alive and violated
They lay on their beds of ice:
Bivalves: the split bulb
And philandering sigh of ocean.
Millions of them ripped and shucked and scattered.

We had driven to the coast
Through flowers and limestone
And there we were, toasting friendship,
Laying down a perfect memory
In the cool of thatch and crockery.

Over the Alps, packed deep in hay and snow,
The Romans hauled their oysters south to Rome:
I saw damp panniers disgorge
The frond-lipped, brine-stung
Glut of privilege

And was angry that my trust could not repose
In the clear light, like poetry or freedom
Leaning in from sea. I ate the day
Deliberately, that its tang
Might quicken me all into verb, pure verb.

1979

Dream Song #90

Op. posth. no. 13

In the night-reaches dreamed he of better graces,
of liberations, and beloved faces,
such as now ere dawn he sings.
It would not be easy, accustomed to these things,
to give up the old world, but he could try;
let it all rest, have a good cry.

Let Randall rest, whom your self-torturing
cannot restore one instant's good to, rest:
he's left us now.
The panic died and in the panic's dying
so did my old friend. I am headed west
also, also, somehow.

In the chambers of the end we'll meet again
I will say Randall, he'll say Pussycat
and all will be as before
whenas we sought, among the beloved faces,
eminence and were dissatisfied with that
and needed more.

1968

Dream Song #149

The world is gradually becoming a place
where I do not care to be any more. Can Delmore die?
I don't suppose
in all them years a day went ever by
without a loving thought for him. Welladay.
In the brightness of his promise,

unstained, I saw him thro' the mist of the actual
blazing with insight, warm with gossip
thro' all our Harvard years
when both of us were just becoming known
I got him out of a police-station once, in Washington, the world is *tref*
and grief too astray for tears.

I imagine you have heard the terrible news,
that Delmore Schwartz is dead, miserably & alone,
in New York: he sang me a song
"I am the Brooklyn poet Delmore Schwartz
Harms & the child I sing, two parents' torts"
when he was young & gift-strong.

1968

Epilogue

Those blessed structures, plot and rhyme—
why are they no help to me now
I want to make
something imagined, not recalled?
I hear the noise of my own voice:
The painter's vision is not a lens,
it trembles to caress the light.
But sometimes everything I write
with the threadbare art of my eye
seems a snapshot,
lurid, rapid, garish, grouped,
heightened from life,
yet paralyzed by fact.
All's misalliance.
Yet why not say what happened?
Pray for the grace of accuracy
Vermeer gave to the sun's illumination
stealing like the tide across a map
to his girl solid with yearning.
We are poor passing facts,
warned by that to give
each figure in the photograph
his living name.

1977

THE
1980s AND 1990s

ELIZABETH BISHOP

North Haven

in memoriam: Robert Lowell

I can make out the rigging of a schooner
a mile off; I can count
the new cones on the spruce. It is so still
the pale bay wears a milky skin, the sky
no clouds, except for one long, carded horse's-tail.

The islands haven't shifted since last summer,
even if I like to pretend they have
—drifting, in a dreamy sort of way,
a little north, a little south or sidewise,
and that they're free within the blue frontiers of bay.

This month, our favorite one is full of flowers:
Buttercups, Red Clover, Purple Vetch,
Hawkweed still burning, Daisies pied, Eyebright,
the Fragrant Bedstraw's incandescent stars,
and more, returned, to paint the meadows with delight.

The Goldfinches are back, or others like them,
and the White-throated Sparrow's five-note song,
pleading and pleading, brings tears to the eyes.
Nature repeats herself, or almost does:
repeat, repeat, repeat; revise, revise, revise.

Years ago, you told me it was here
(in 1932?) you first "discovered *girls*"
and learned to sail, and learned to kiss.
You had "such fun," you said, that classic summer.
("Fun"—it always seemed to leave you at a loss . . .)

You left North Haven, anchored in its rock,
afloat in mystic blue . . . And now—you've left
for good. You can't derange, or re-arrange,
your poems again. (But the Sparrows can their song.)
The words won't change again. Sad friend, you cannot change.

1983

SEAMUS HEANEY

Clearances, III

When all the others were away at Mass
I was all hers as we peeled potatoes.
They broke the silence, let fall one by one
Like solder weeping off the soldering iron:
Cold comforts set between us, things to share
Gleaming in a bucket of clean water.
And again let fall. Little pleasant splashes
From each other's work would bring us to our senses.

So while the parish priest at her bedside
Went hammer and tongs at the prayers for the dying
And some were responding and some crying
I remembered her head bent towards my head,
Her breath in mine, our fluent dipping knives—
Never closer the whole rest of our lives.

1987

The Ball Poem

What is the boy now, who has lost his ball,
What, what is he to do? I saw it go
Merrily bouncing, down the street, and then
Merrily over—there it is in the water!
No use to say "O there are other balls":
An ultimate shaking grief fixes the boy
As he stands rigid, trembling, staring down
All his young days into the harbour where
His ball went. I would not intrude on him,
A dime, another ball, is worthless. Now
He senses first responsibility
In a world of possessions. People will take balls,
Balls will be lost always, little boy,
And no one buys a ball back. Money is external.
He is learning, well behind his desperate eyes,
The epistemology of loss, how to stand up
Knowing what every man must one day know
And most know many days, how to stand up
And gradually light returns to the street,
A whistle blows, the ball is out of sight,
Soon part of me will explore the deep and dark
Floor of the harbour . . . I am everywhere,
I suffer and move, my mind and my heart move
With all that move me, under the water
Or whistling, I am not a little boy.

1989

STEVIE SMITH

On the Dressing gown lent me by my Hostess the Brazilian Consul in Milan, 1958

Dear Daughter of the Southern Cross
I admit your fiery nature and your loss

Your fiery integrity and your intelligence
I admit your high post and its relevance

And I admit, dear Consuelessa, that your dressing gown
Has wrapped me from the offences of the town

From rain in Milan in a peculiar May
From anger at break of day
From heat and cold as I lay

Wrapped me, but not entirely, from the words I must hear
Thrown between you and him, that were not "dear".

Oh that him
Was a problem
Consuelessa, your husband.

He and I ran together in the streets, I think
We grew more English with each drink
And we laughed as we ran in the town
Consuelessa, where then was your dressing gown?

The Portuguese and Italian languages
Drew our laughter in stages
Of infantine rages,
This was outrageous.

Yes, I admit your courage, I heard
Heart steel at the word
That found everything absurd,
The English word I spoke and heard.

Tapping at your heels, Consuelessa,
We were children again, your husband and I,
A worthless couple,

Hanging behind, whining, being slow,
"Where is our wife?" we cry. (This you knew.)
"Give us money" we said, "you have not given us much".
We were your kiddies, Consuelessa, out for a touch.

Yet I admit your dressing gown
Wrapped me from the offences of the town
But never from my own
Ah Consuelessa, this I own.

From rain in May
From the cold as I lay
When the servant Cesare had stolen
The electric fire, the only one,
From disappointment too I dare say
Consuelessa,
It is your dressing gown I remember today.

1982

Song

The light lies layered in the leaves.
Trees, and trees, more trees.
A cloud boy brings the evening paper:
The Evening Sun. It sets.
Not sharply or at once
a stately progress down the sky
(it's gilt and pink and faintly green)
above, beyond, behind the evening leaves
of trees. Traffic sounds and
bells resound in silver clangs
the hour, a tune, my friend
Pierrot. The violet hour:
the grass is violent green.
A weeping beech is gray,
a copper beech is copper red.
Tennis nets hang
unused in unused stillness.
A car starts up and
whispers into what will soon be night.
A tennis ball is served.
A horsefly vanishes.
A smoking cigarette.
A day (so many and so few)
dies down a hardened sky
and leaves are lap-held notebook leaves
discriminated barely
in light no longer layered.

1980

Sleepless City

(Brooklyn Bridge Nocturne)

Out in the sky, no one sleeps. No one, no one.
No one sleeps.
Lunar creatures sniff and circle the dwellings.
Live iguanas will come to bite the men who don't dream,
and the brokenhearted fugitive will meet on street corners
an incredible crocodile resting beneath the tender protest of the stars.

Out in the world, no one sleeps. No one, no one.
No one sleeps.
There is a corpse in the farthest graveyard
complaining for three years
because of an arid landscape in his knee;
and a boy who was buried this morning cried so much
they had to call the dogs to quiet him.

Life is no dream. Watch out! Watch out! Watch out!
We fall down stairs and eat the moist earth,
or we climb to the snow's edge with the choir of dead dahlias.
But there is no oblivion, no dream:
raw flesh. Kisses tie mouths
in a tangle of new veins
and those in pain will bear it with no respite
and those who are frightened by death will carry it on their shoulders.

One day
horses will live in the taverns
and furious ants
will attack the yellow skies that take refuge in the eyes of cattle.

Another day
we'll witness the resurrection of dead butterflies,
and even when walking in a landscape of gray sponges and silent ships,
we'll see our ring shine and roses spill from our tongues.
Watch out! Watch out! Watch out!
Those still marked by claws and cloudburst,
that boy who cries because he doesn't know bridges exist,
or that corpse that has nothing more than its head and one shoe—
they all must be led to the wall where iguanas and serpents wait,
where the bear's teeth wait,
where the mummified hand of a child waits
and the camel's fur bristles with a violent blue chill.

Out in the sky, no one sleeps. No one, no one.
No one sleeps.
But if someone closes his eyes,
whip him, my children, whip him!
Let there be a panorama of open eyes
and bitter inflamed wounds.
Out in the world, no one sleeps. No one. No one.
I've said it before.
No one sleeps.
But at night, if someone has too much moss on his temples,
open the trap doors so he can see in moonlight
the fake goblets, the venom, and the skull of the theaters.

1988

Translated by Greg Simon and Steven F. White

Walking

At dusk the world smells of iodine.
The mountain creaks like a ship's mast;
but you, without even thinking about it,
surrounded by tree trunks, know that at this hour
the sea goes into its nest of dry old straw.

How fine that you have so much sea in you
and so much light and so much blue in the visor
of your worn cap!
And that you can walk through these fields
sunk in the whispering swells of the leaves.
Hailstones and rocks have fallen on your years,
spilling them out in downpours.
You love this field, these rocks and brambles,
flowers, beasts, birds of this country,
love in this land everything you know and everything
        you don't know,
love even the thorn that scratches you,
and want that twisted palm on the hill to love you,
because neither lightning strokes nor cyclones have been able
        to fell it,
because it is oppressed by the hard summer
until night smothers its flames,
but the green fronds, high in the wind, rise above the fire,
and the trunk, though blackened, nourishes them and
        sustains them.

1982

Translated by Alastair Reid

"Above the Inland Empire today"

Above the Inland Empire today the sky is off the desert, deceptively active in a ridiculous heat. The whole country is hot, colored red-orange on the news. We are stuck here on earth with no breath of air. Coolers rumble all over town; I actually consider making lemonade. If there is a remedy, I will stay.

I was born into my skin and its future, the planet and its promise or demise. Each day a similar sun, the almost predictable moods of the moon, seasonal weather holding its shape for planned vacations.

After the earthquake this morning, the day broke sizzling with monstrous clouds to the east—what Mama once called "earthquake weather." I stood in the doorway until the windows quieted, and went back to bed, sleeping easily, rocking, anchored through dreams to the shifting plate. I trust the blatant forces, and worry only about that which grows and moves unseen, the odd cell, thriving.

Eileen, there is no way to practice traveling alone; you just go. And you might finally hear for yourself the stories you told us from your sleep. Maybe. Doesn't seem to matter how hard you try, you don't leave when you intended, and it's the idea of a cure, the reassurance of your own power, that defeats you. The world fails and you are a failure—not finding the impossible recovery that was set for you.

All disasters are natural. The heart shudders; the flood fills. No one knows what to die of.

1989

LES MURRAY

Water-Gardening in an Old Farm Dam

Blueing the blackened water
that I'm widening with my spade
as I lever up water tussocks
and chuck them ashore like sopping comets
is a sun-point, dazzling heatless
acetylene, under tadpoles that swarm
wobbling, like a species of flies
and buzzing bubbles that speed
upward like many winged species.

Unwettable green tacos are lotus leaves.
Waterlily leaves are notches plaques
of the water. Their tubers resemble
charred monstera trunks. Some I planted,
some I let float. And I bought
thumb-sized mosquito-eating fish
for a dollar in a plastic amnion.
"Wilderness" says we've lost belief
in human building: our dominance
now so complete that we hide from it.

Where, with my levered back,
I stand, too late in life,
in a populous amber, feet deep
in digesting chyle over clays,
I love green humanised water
in old brick pounds, water carried
unleaking for miles around contour,
or built out into, or overstepping
stonework in long frilled excess.

The hands' pride and abysmal
pay that such labour earned,
as against the necks and billions
paid for Nature. But the workers
and the need are gone, without reaching
here: this was never canal country.
It's cow-ceramic, softened at rain times,
where the kookaburra's laugh
is like angles of a scrubbing toothbrush
heard through the bones of the head.

Level water should turn out of sight,
on round a bend, behind an island,
in windings of possibility, not
be exhausted in one gesture, like an avenue.
It shouldn't be surveyable in one look.
That's a waterhole. Still, the trees
I planted along this one bend it
a bit, and half roof it, bringing
its wet underearth shadow to the surface
as shade. And the reeds I hate,

mint sheaves, human-high palisades
that would close in round the water,
I could fire floating petrol among them
again, and savage but not beat them,
or I could declare them beautiful.

1997

DEREK WALCOTT

Gros-Ilet

From this village, soaked like a gray rag in salt water,
a language came, garnished with conch shells,
with a suspicion of berries in its armpits
and elbows like flexible oars. Every ceremony commenced
in the troughs, in the middens, at the daybreak and the daydark funerals
attended by crabs. The odors were fortified
by the sea. The anchor of the islands went deep
but was always clear in the sand. Many a shark,
and often the ray, whose wings are as wide as sails,
rose with insomniac stare from the wavering corals,
and a fisherman held up a catfish like a tendriled head.
And the night with its certain, inextinguishable candles
was like All Souls' Night upside down, the way a bat keeps
its own view of the world. So their eyes looked down, amused,
on us, and found we were walking strangely,
and wondered about our sense of balance, how we slept
as if we were dead, how we confused
dreams with ordinary things like nails, or roses,
how rocks aged quickly with moss,
the sea made furrows that had nothing to do with time,
and the sand started whirlwinds with nothing to do at all,
and the shadows answered to the sun alone.
And sometimes, like the top of an old tire,
the black rim of a porpoise. Elpenor, you
who broke your arse, drunk, tumbling down the bulkhead,
and the steersman who sails, like the ray under the breathing waves,
keep moving, there is nothing here for you.
There are different candles and customs here, the dead
are different. Different shells guard their graves.
There are distinctions beyond the paradise

of our horizon. This is not the grape-purple Aegean.
There is no wine here, no cheese, the almonds are green,
the sea grapes bitter, the language is that of slaves.

1987

The Whitsun Weddings

That Whitsun, I was late getting away:
    Not till about
One-twenty on the sunlit Saturday
Did my three-quarters-empty train pull out,
All windows down, all cushions hot, all sense
Of being in a hurry gone. We ran
Behind the backs of houses, crossed a street
Of blinding windscreens, smelt the fish-dock; thence
The river's level drifting breadth began,
Where sky and Lincolnshire and water meet.

All afternoon, through the tall heat that slept
    For miles inland,
A slow and stopping curve southwards we kept.
Wide farms went by, short-shadowed cattle, and
Canals with floatings of industrial froth;
A hothouse flashed uniquely: hedges dipped
And rose: and now and then a smell of grass
Displaced the reek of buttoned carriage-cloth
Until the next town, new and nondescript,
Approached with acres of dismantled cars.

At first, I didn't notice what a noise
    The weddings made
Each station that we stopped at: sun destroys
The interest of what's happening in the shade,
And down the long cool platforms whoops and skirls
I took for porters larking with the mails,
And went on reading. Once we started, though,
We passed them, grinning and pomaded, girls

In parodies of fashion, heels and veils,
All posed irresolutely, watching us go,

As if out on the end of an event
    Waving goodbye
To something that survived it. Struck, I leant
More promptly out next time, more curiously,
And saw it all again in different terms:
The fathers with broad belts under their suits
And seamy foreheads; mothers loud and fat;
An uncle shouting smut; and then the perms,
The nylon gloves and jewellery-substitutes,
The lemons, mauves, and olive-ochres that

Marked off the girls unreally from the rest.
    Yes, from cafés
And banquet-halls up yards, and bunting-dressed
Coach-party annexes, the wedding-days
Were coming to an end. All down the line
Fresh couples climbed aboard: the rest stood round;
The last confetti and advice were thrown,
And, as we moved, each face seemed to define
Just what it saw departing: children frowned
At something dull; fathers had never known

Success so huge and wholly farcical;
    The women shared
The secret like a happy funeral;
While girls, gripping their handbags tighter, stared
At a religious wounding. Free at last,
And loaded with the sum of all they saw,
We hurried towards London, shuffling gouts of steam.
Now fields were building-plots, and poplars cast
Long shadows over major roads, and for
Some fifty minutes, that in time would seem

Just long enough to settle hats and say
    I nearly died,
A dozen marriages got under way.
They watched the landscape, sitting side by side
—An Odeon went past, a cooling tower,
And someone running up to bowl—and none
Thought of the others they would never meet
Or how their lives would all contain this hour.
I thought of London spread out in the sun,
Its postal districts packed like squares of wheat:

There we were aimed. And as we raced across
    Bright knots of rail
Past standing Pullmans, walls of blackened moss
Came close, and it was nearly done, this frail
Travelling coincidence; and what it held
Stood ready to be loosed with all the power
That being changed can give. We slowed again,
And as the tightened brakes took hold, there swelled
A sense of falling, like an arrow-shower
Sent out of sight, somewhere becoming rain.

1989

JOSEPH BRODSKY

To Urania

To I.K.

Everything has its limit, including sorrow.
A windowpane stalls a stare. Nor does a grille abandon
a leaf. One may rattle the keys, gurgle down a swallow.
Loneliness cubes a man at random.
A camel sniffs at the rail with a resentful nostril;
a perspective cuts emptiness deep and even.
And what is space anyway if not the
body's absence at every given
point? That's why Urania's older than sister Clio!
In daylight or with the soot-rich lantern,
you see the globe's pate free of any bio,
you see she hides nothing, unlike the latter.
There they are, blueberry-laden forests,
rivers where the folk with bare hands catch sturgeon
or the towns in whose soggy phone books
you are starring no longer; father eastward surge on
brown mountain ranges; wild mares carousing
in tall sedge; the cheekbones get yellower
as they turn numerous. And still farther east, steam dreadnoughts or cruisers,
and the expanse grows blue like lace underwear.

1988

ADAM ZAGAJEWSKI

Russia Comes into Poland

For Joseph Brodsky

Through meadow and hedgerow, village and forest,
cavalries on the march, infantries on the march,
horses and cannons, old soldiers, young soldiers, children,
wiry wolfhounds at full gallop, a blizzard of feathers,
sleds, Black Marias, carriages, taxis,
even the old cars called Moskwitch come roaring in,
and warships and rafts and pontoon bridges roar in,
and barges, steamships, canoes (some of which sink),
barrage balloons, missiles, bombers,
howitzer shells whistling arias from an opera,
the shriek of flagellants and the growl of commands,
songs slashing the air with notes made of steel,
yurts and tents break camp, ropes tighten,
banners of dyed linen tremble overhead.
Messengers, painting, die as they run,
cables rush out, candles burning with quick crimson flames,
colonels dozing in carriages faster than light,
popes piously murmuring blessings,
even the moon is along on that hard, iron march.
Tanks, sabers, ropes,
Katyusha shells whirring like comets,
fifes and drums exploding the air,
·clubs crunching, the heaving decks of ferries
and of invasions sigh, sway, the sons of the steppes
on the march, Moslems, condemned prisoners, lovers
of Byron, gamblers, the whole progeny
of Asia with Suvorov in the lead

limps in with a train of fawning courtiers who dance;
the yellow Volga runs in, Siberian rivers chanting,
camels pensively plod, bringing
the sands of the desert and humid mirages,
the fold-eyed Kirghizes marching in step,
the black pupils of the God of the Urals,
and behind them schoolteachers and languages straggle,
and behind them old manor houses skate in like gliders,
and German doctors with dressings and plasters;
the wounded with their alabaster faces,
regiments and divisions, cavalries, infantries, on the march,
Russia comes into Poland,
tearing cobwebs, leaves, silk ribbons,
ligaments and frontiers,
breaking
treaties, bridges, alliances,
threads, ties, clotheslines with wet washing still waving,
gates, arteries, bandages and conjunctions,
future and hope;
Russia comes in, marching
into a hamlet on the Pilica,
into the deep Mazovia forests,
rending posters and parliaments,
trampling roads, footbridges, paths, streams.
Russia comes into the eighteenth century,
into October, September, laughter and tears,
into conscience, into the concentration
of the student, the calm silence of the warm bricks of a wall,
comes into the fragrance
of meadows, herbs, the tangled paths of the forest,
trampling
the pansy, the wild rose,
hoofprints in the moss, tractor and tank prints
in the soft moss,
it overturns

chimneys, tree trunks, palaces,

turns off lights, makes great bonfires

out in the formal garden,

stains the clear spring,

razes the library, church, town hall,

flooding its scarlet banners through the sky,

Russia comes into my life,

Russia comes into my thought,

Russia comes into my poetry.

1991

Translated by Renata Gorczynski, Benjamin Ivry, and C. K. Williams

Poem Does

The god in the nitroglycerin
Is speedily absorbed under the tongue
Till it turns a green man red,
Which is what a poem does.
It explosively reanimates
By oxygenating the tribe.

No civilized state will execute
Someone who is ill
Till it makes the someone well
Enough to kill
In a civilized state,
As a poem does.

I run-and-bump the tiny
Honda 125cc Grand Prix racer. Only
Two steps and it screams. I
Slip the clutch to get the revs up, blipping and getting
Ready not to get deady,
Which also is what a poem does.

They dress them up in the retirement centers.
They dress them up in racing leathers.
They dress them up in war paint and feathers.
The autumn trees are in their gory glory.
The logs in the roaring fire keep passing
The peace pipe in pain, just what a poem does.

Stanza no. 5. We want to be alive.

Line 26. We pray for peace.

Line 27. The warrior and peacemaker Rabin is in heaven.

28. We don't accept his fate.

But we do. Life is going ahead as fast as it can,

Which is what a poem does.

1998

What Ails My Fern?

My peonies have lovely leaves
but rarely flower.
Oh, they have buds
and plenty of them. These
grow to the size of peas
and stay
that way.
Is this
bud blast?

What ails my fern?
I enclose a sample
of a white disease
on a leaf
of honesty
known also
as the money plant

My two blue spruce
look worse and worse

What ails my fern?

Two years ago a tenant
wound tape around my tree.
Sap dripped out of the branches
on babies in buggies below. So
I unwound the tape.
Can nothing be done
to revive my tree?

What ails my fern?

I hate my disordered
backyard fence
where lilac, weigela
and mock orange grow.
Please advise
how to get rid of it.

Weeping willow roots
reaching out
seeking water
fill my cesspool and well.
What do you suggest?

What ails my fern?

1993

JOHN ASHBERY

The Problem of Anxiety

Fifty years have passed
since I started living in those dark towns
I was telling you about.
Well, not much has changed. I still can't figure out
how to get from the post office to the swings in the park.
Apple trees blossom in the cold, not from conviction,
and my hair is the color of dandelion fluff.

Suppose this poem were about you—would *you*
put in the things I've carefully left out:
descriptions of pain, and sex, and how shiftily
people behave toward each other? Naw, that's
all in some book it seems. For you
I've saved the descriptions of chicken sandwiches,
and the glass eye that stares at me in amazement
from the bronze mantel, and will never be appeased.

1995

Santarém

Of course I may be remembering it all wrong
after, after—how many years?

That golden evening I really wanted to go no farther;
more than anything else I wanted to stay awhile
in that conflux of two great rivers, Tapajós, Amazon,
grandly, silently flowing, flowing east.
Suddenly there'd been houses, people, and lots of mongrel
riverboats skittering back and forth
under a sky of gorgeous, under-lit clouds,
with everything gilded, burnished along one side,
and everything bright, cheerful, casual—or so it looked.
I liked the place; I liked the idea of the place.
Two rivers. Hadn't two rivers sprung
from the Garden of Eden? No, that was four
and they'd diverged. Here only two
and coming together. Even if one were tempted
to literary interpretations
such as: life/death, right/wrong, male/female
—such notions would have resolved, dissolved, straight off
in that watery, dazzling dialectic.

In front of the church, the Cathedral, rather,
there was a modest promenade and a belvedere
about to fall into the river,
stubby palms, flamboyants like pans of embers,
buildings one story high, stucco, blue or yellow,
and one house faced with *azulejos*, buttercup yellow.
The street was deep in dark-gold river sand
damp from the ritual afternoon rain,

and teams of zebus plodded, gentle, proud,
and *blue*, with down-curved horns and hanging ears,
pulling carts with solid wheels.
The zebus' hooves, the people's feet
waded in golden sand,
dampened by golden sand,
so that almost the only sounds
were creaks and *shush, shush, shush.*

Two rivers full of crazy shipping—people
all apparently changing their minds, embarking,
disembarking, rowing clumsy dories.
(After the Civil War some Southern families
came here; here they could still own slaves.
They left occasional blue eyes, English names,
and *oars*. No other place, no one
on all the Amazon's four thousand miles
does anything but paddle.)
A dozen or so young nuns, white-habited,
waved gaily from an old stern-wheeler
getting up steam, already hung with hammocks
—off to their mission, days and days away
up God knows what lost tributary.
Side-wheelers, countless wobbling dugouts . . .
A cow stood up in one, quite calm,
chewing her cud while being ferried,
tipping, wobbling, somewhere, to be married.
A river schooner with raked masts
and violet-colored sails tacked in so close
her bowsprit seemed to touch the church

(Cathedral, rather!). A week or so before
there'd been a thunderstorm and the Cathedral'd
been struck by lightning. One tower had
a widening zigzag crack all the way down.
It was a miracle. The priest's house right next door

had been struck, too, and his brass bed
(the only one in town) galvanized black.
Graças a deus—he'd been in Belém.

In the blue pharmacy the pharmacist
had hung an empty wasps' nest from a shelf:
small, exquisite, clean matte white,
and hard as stucco. I admired it
so much he gave it to me.
Then—my ship's whistle blew. I couldn't stay.
Back on board, a fellow-passenger, Mr. Swan,
Dutch, the retiring head of Philips Electric,
really a very nice old man,
who wanted to see the Amazon before he died,
asked, "What's that ugly thing?"

1983

AUGUST KLEINZAHLER

Green Sees Things in Waves

Green first thing each day sees waves—
the chair, armoire, overhead fixtures, you name it,
waves—which, you might say, things really are,
but Green just lies there awhile breathing
long slow breaths, in and out, through his mouth
like he was maybe seasick, until in an hour or so
the waves simmer down and then the trails and colors
off of things, that all quiets down as well and Green
starts to think of washing up, breakfast even
with everything still moving around, colors, trails,
and sounds, from the street and plumbing next door,
vibrating—of course you might say that's what
sound really is, after all, vibrations—but Green,
he's not thinking physics at this stage, nuh-uh,
our boy's only trying to get himself out of bed,
get a grip, but sometimes, and this is the kicker,
another party, shall we say, is in the room
with Green, and Green knows this other party
and they do *not* get along, which understates it
quite a bit, quite a bit, and Green knows
that this other cat is an hallucination, right,
but these two have a routine that goes way back
and Green starts hollering, throwing stuff
until he's all shook up, whole day gone to hell,
bummer . . .
       Anyhow, the docs are having a look,
see if they can't dream up a cocktail,
but seems our boy ate quite a pile of acid one time,
clinical, wow, enough juice for half a block—

go go go, little Greenie—blew the wiring out
from behind his headlights and now, no matter what,
can't find the knob to turn off the show.

1998

C. K. WILLIAMS

Garden

A garden I usually never would visit; oaks, roses, the scent of roses I usually
wouldn't remark

but do now, in a moment for no reason suddenly unlike any other, numinous,
limpid, abundant,

whose serenity lifts and enfolds me, as a swirl of breeze lifts the leaves and
enfolds them.

Nothing ever like this, not even love, though there's no need to measure, no
need to compare:

for once not to be waiting, to be in the world as time moves through and
across me,

to exult in this fragrant light given to me, in this flow of warmth given to
me and the world.

Then, on my hand beside me on the bench, something, I thought somebody
else's hand, alighted;

I flinched it off, and saw—sorrow!—a warbler, gray, black, yellow, in flight
already away.

It stopped near me in a shrub, though, and waited, as though unstartled, as
though unafraid,

as though to tell me my reflex of fear was no failure, that if I believed I had
lost something,

I was wrong, because nothing can be lost, of the self, of a lifetime of
bringing forth selves.

Then it was gone, its branch springing back empty: still oak, though, still
rose, still world.

1997

SAPPHO

"Artfully adorned Aphrodite, deathless"

Artfully adorned Aphrodite, deathless
child of Zeus and weaver of wiles I beg you
please don't hurt me, don't overcome my spirit,
  goddess, with longing,

but come here, if ever at other moments
hearing these my words from afar you listened
and responded: leaving your father's house, all
  golden, you came then,

hitching up your chariot: lovely sparrows
drew you quickly over the dark earth, whirling
on fine beating wings from the heights of heaven
  down through the sky and

instantly arrived—and then O my blessed
goddess with a smile on your deathless face you
asked me what the matter was *this* time, what I
  called you for this time,

what I now most wanted to happen in my
raving heart: "Whom *this* time should I persuade to
lead you back again to her love? Who *now*, oh
  Sappho, who wrongs you?

If she flees you now, she will soon pursue you;
if she won't accept what you give, she'll give it;
if she doesn't love you, she'll love you soon now,
  even unwilling."

Come to me again, and release me from this
want past bearing. All that my heart desires to
happen—make it happen. And stand beside me,
    goddess, my ally.

1993

Translated by Jim Powell

Guilty of Dust

up or down from the infinite C E N T E R
B R I M M I N G at the winking rim of time

the voice in my head said

LOVE IS THE DISTANCE
BETWEEN YOU AND WHAT YOU LOVE

WHAT YOU LOVE IS YOUR FATE

    *

then I saw the parade of my loves

those PERFORMERS comics actors singers

forgetful of my very self so often I
desired to die to myself to live in them

then my PARENTS my FRIENDS the drained
SPECTRES once filled with my baffled infatuations

love and guilt and fury and
sweetness for whom

nail spirit yearning to the earth

    *

then the voice in my head said

WHETHER YOU LOVE WHAT YOU LOVE

OR LIVE IN DIVIDED CEASELESS
REVOLT AGAINST IT

WHAT YOU LOVE IS YOUR FATE

1990

Before Our Eyes

The sky almost transparent, saturated
manganese blue. Windy and cold.
A yellow line beside a black line,
the chimney on the roof a yellow line
behind the mountain ash on Horatio.
A circular cut of pink flesh hanging
in the shop. Fish, flattened, copper,
heads chopped off. The point is to bring
depths to the surface, to elevate
sensuous experience into speech
and the social contract. Ribbons of smoke
silhouette the pier, a navy of yachts
pounded by the river's green waves.
By written I mean made, by made I mean felt;
concealed things, sweet sleep of colors.
So you will be, perhaps appropriately,
dismissed for it, a morality of seeing,
laying it on. Who among the idealists
won't sit in the private domain,
exchange culture with the moneymakers?
Here's one with acute hypertension
ready to crack the pressure cuff,
there's the type whose hallucinatory
devolution of the history of tribes
is personalized. My grandpa? He never
contended where Lebanon's history
began, if the child prince was smuggled
by his mother to a Catholic family
in the Mountain where he passed his boyhood
in his father's religion, a Druse,

the most secret sect of Islam.
I received the news in Jerusalem—
the Beirut Easter radio event, the dancer
undulating to sounds of explosions
outside the studio. The future isn't Africa,
my friend, and Europe's a peninsula of Asia,
and your America's a creation of Europe,
he laughed, the newspaperman, pointing
his finger. Still, don't street smarts
matter? Waiting rooms, shopping centers,
after all, empty moods and emotions.
And no denial's built up inside me.
It was, I admit, more charged than
I thought at the time. More predetermined.
Silver and red scraps inside the air,
cascades of sublimated pig iron.
Language more discursive, a more sequential
expression, and I attested to it.
The old dying? The new not yet born? The old,
the new, you fool, aphorized by Henry Ford
in '22. First make the cars, the roads
will follow. Modes of production created
of their own accord. The process runs
of its own accord. Current and diaphanous
sight and sound, comprehended, but poetry
I know something about. The act of forming
imagined language resisting humiliation.
Fading browns and reds, a maroon glow,
sadness and brightness, glorified.
Voices over charred embankments, smell
of fire and fat. The pure metamorphic
rush through with senses, just as you said
it would be. The soft, subtle twilight
only the bearer feels, broken into angles,
best kept to oneself. For the time being
let's just keep to what's before our eyes.

1993

Six Belons

The ruckled lips gaped slightly, but when
I slipped the knife in next to the hinge,
they closed to a stone.
The violence it took to unlock them!
Each wounded thing lay in opalescent milk
like an albino heart,
muscle sliced from the roof-shell.
I took each one pale and harmless
into my mouth and held it there,
tasting the difference between
the ligament and the pure, faintly
coffee-colored flesh that was unflinching
even in the acid of lemon juice,
so that I felt I was eating
not the body but the life in the body.
Afterward my mouth stayed greedy
though it carried the sea-rankness
away with it, a taste usually transient,
held for a moment beyond its time
on mustache or fingertip.
The shells looked abruptly old,
crudely fluted, gray-green, flecked
with the undersea equivalent of lichens,
and pearly, slick, bereft of all their meat.
The creatures themselves were gone,
the succulent indecent briny ghosts
that caused this arousal, this feeding,
and now a sudden loneliness.

1991

Changing at York

A directory that runs from B to V,
the Yellow Pages' entries for HOTELS
and TAXIS torn out, the smell of dossers' pee,
saliva in the mouthpiece, whisky smells—
I remember, now that I have to phone,
squashing a *Daily Mail* half full of chips,
to tell the son I left at home alone
my train's delayed, and get cut off by the pips,
how, phoning his mother, late, a little pissed,
changing at York, from some place where I'd read,
I used 2p to lie about the train I'd missed
and ten more to talk my way to some girl's bed
and, in this same kiosk with the stale, sour breath
of queuing callers, drunk, cajoling, lying,
consoling his grandpa for his granny's death,
how I heard him, for the first time ever, crying.

1990

from *Cora Fry's Pillow Book*

"I go to work because it pays."

I go to work because it pays.
I go to work to get away.
I go to work to change my face.
I go to work to wash my hands
and wear a wig to save my head.
(I leave mine home.)
I go to work to be unknown
and in the kitchen sweating rain
I put a heavy tray down full

and watch the new man watching me.
What messages between his eyes
and mine there's room for here. . . . He's thin
as someone's undernourished son.
If I go ask for some glasses,
depending on my voice and where
my shoulders are, compared to his,
I could make room on his pillow
for my head, with or without wig.
I move my tray the other way.

Felice moves then, smiling her gap-
tooth grin. Her thighs, I think, open
and close, mouth breathing mostly in,
chattering at men endlessly,
wanting to be shut, not sweetly.

Felice has stopped two babies quick.
Times she thought they were taking care.
"Don't trust them, Core, with a blind nun.
They could care less. No matter how
they watch your ass, it's yours to watch."

1994

The Decanter

Wonder of wonders! Water's limpid sphere
is kept from falling by a glass decanter.
Where does it come from? How did it appear
in this huge institution? As I stand here
transfixed beside the table, wondering which
gray, predawn park we had till now forgotten,
I'm happy knowing water's shape can switch,
always submissive to the form it's caught in.
And the decanter, out of emptiness,
floats like the ghost of an ice floe that melted
or like the answer to a dreamed request
by the unlucky dead whom thirst has wilted.

Having picked up a glass, should I now start
to take a sip, and feel how I can't stop its
arresting chill from spreading to the heart
unbearable compassion for all objects?
When I've talked with a girl from down the hall,
I'll sigh; you'd think she caused it, but it's not her.
No; separated by an unseen wall,
they're looking at each other: air and water.

1991

Translated by Paul Graves and Carol Ueland

Brancusi's Golden Bird

The toy
become the aesthetic archetype

As if

some patient peasant God
had rubbed and rubbed
the Alpha and Omega
of Form
into a lump of metal

A naked orientation
unwinged   unplumed
    —the ultimate rhythm
has lopped the extremities
of crest and claw
from
the nucleus of flight

The absolute act
of art
conformed
to continent sculpture
—bare as the brow of Osiris—
this breast of revelation

an incandescent curve
licked by chromatic flames
in labyrinths of reflections

This gong
of polished hyperaesthesia
shrills with brass
as the aggressive light
strikes
its significance

The immaculate
conception
of the inaudible bird
occurs
in gorgeous reticence   .   .   .

1996

GJERTRUD SCHNACKENBERG

A Gilded Lapse of Time

(Ravenna)

1. THE MAUSOLEUM OF GALLA PLACIDIA

When love was driven back upon itself,
When a lapse, where my life should have been,
Opened like a breach in the wall, and I stood
At a standstill before the gate built with mud,
I thought my name was spoken and I couldn't reply—
Even knowing that when you hear your name
It's a soul on the other side who is grieving
For you, though you're never told why.

Among the hallowed statues of dead stalks
I stood, where the rosebush was abandoned by
The pruning shears, among the stumps of brambles
Near the muddy door to the next life.
There was a rubbish mound at the ancient gate
And a broken branch the gardeners had tossed
Toward the leaf pile, scattering its gold dust
Before the doorway carved, as if into a hillside,
Into a frozen room raised in the desolate
Outskirts of Byzantium, where now an industrial zone
Pressed toward the porch of an ancient church
Built in the fulfillment of a vow,
Where the Byzantines would lay aside
Their musical instruments in order to enter
The sanctuary unaccompanied; I stood

Uncertain at the threshold of a pile
Of enigmatic, rose-colored brick, a tomb
A barbarian empress built for herself
That conceals within its inauspicious,
Shattered-looking vault the whirl of gold,
The inflooding realm we may only touch
For one instant with a total leap of the heart—
Like the work of the bees who laid aside
Their holy, inner craft because the Lord
Whistled for them, and they fled
To Him, but long ago, leaving behind
These unfinished combs from biblical antiquity
We are forbidden to touch, still deep
In the wood's heart, still dripping on the ground.

1992

JAMES WRIGHT

As I Step over a Puddle at the End of Winter, I Think of an Ancient Chinese Governor

And how can I, born in evil days
And fresh from failure, ask a kindness of Fate?

—WRITTEN A.D. 819

Po Chu-i, balding old politician,
What's the use?
I think of you,
Uneasily entering the gorges of the Yang-Tze,
When you were being towed up the rapids
Toward some political job or other
In the city of Chungshou.
You made it, I guess,
By dark.

But it is 1960, it is almost spring again,
And the tall rocks of Minneapolis
Build me my own black twilight
Of bamboo ropes and waters.
Where is Yuan Chen, the friend you loved?
Where is the sea, that once solved the whole loneliness
Of the Midwest? Where is Minneapolis? I can see nothing
But the great terrible oak tree darkening with winter.
Did you find the city of isolated men beyond mountains?
Or have you been holding the end of a frayed rope
For a thousand years?

1990

Japan

Tired and empty,
I occupy a winterized log cabin
In a clearing in a snowy wood
In a country that might be Japan.

Each morning I catechize myself
In the hope that there has been a change
Either from or into the new man
It appears I've partly become.

Lunch arrives in a wicker basket
That later will be taken away.
But when I rush to the window
The encircling snow lies undefiled.

Towards midnight I shall step outside
And expose my face to the stars
And weep, not merely from the cold.
May their beauty appease me.

My best moments are those
When, in default of inspiration,
My hand rests lightly on the wrist
Of the one who writes.

1994

LES MURRAY

The Dream of Wearing Shorts Forever

To go home and wear shorts forever
in the enormous paddocks, in that warm climate,
adding a sweater when winter soaks the grass,

to camp out along the river bends
for good, wearing shorts, with a pocketknife,
a fishing line and matches,

or there where the hills are all down, below the plain,
to sit around in shorts at evening
on the plank verandah—

If the cardinal points of costume
are Robes, Tat, Rig and Scunge,
where are shorts in this compass?

They are never Robes
as other bareleg outfits have been:
the toga, the kilt, the lava-lava
the Mahatma's cotton dhoti;

archbishops and field marshals
at their ceremonies never wear shorts.
The very word
means underpants in North America.

Shorts can be Tat,
Land-Rovering bush-environmental tat,
socio-political ripped-and-metal-stapled tat,
solidarity-with-the-Third-World tat tvam asi,

likewise track-and-field shorts worn to parties
and the further humid, modelling negligée
of the Kingdom of Flaunt,
that unchallenged aristocracy.

More plainly climatic, shorts
are farmers' rig, leathery with salt and bonemeal,
are sailors' and branch bankers' rig,
the crisp golfing style
of our youngest male National Costume.

Most loosely, they are Scunge,
ancient Bengal bloomers or moth-eaten hot pants
worn with a former shirt,
feet, beach sand, hair
and a paucity of signals.

Scunge, which is real negligée
housework in a swimsuit, pyjamas worn all day,
is holiday, is freedom from ambition.
Scunge makes you invisible
to the world and yourself.

The entropy of costume,
scunge can get you conquered by more vigorous cultures
and help you to notice it less.

Satisfied ambition, defeat, true unconcern,
the wish and the knack of self-forgetfulness
all fall within the scunge ambit
wearing board shorts or similar;
it is a kind of weightlessness.

Unlike public nakedness, which in Westerners
is deeply circumstantial, relaxed as exam time,
artless and equal as the corsetry of a hussar regiment,

shorts and their plain like
are an angelic nudity,
spirituality with pockets!
A double updraft as you drop from branch to pool!

Ideal for getting served last
in shops of the temperate zone
they are also ideal for going home, into space,
into time, to farm the mind's Sabine acres
for product and subsistence.

Now that everyone who yearned to wear long pants
has essentially achieved them,
long pants, which have themselves been underwear
repeatedly, and underground more than once,
it is time perhaps to cherish the culture of shorts,

to moderate grim vigour
with the knobble of bare knees,
to cool bareknuckle feet in inland water,
slapping flies with a book on solar wind
or a patient bare hand, beneath the cadjiput trees,

to be walking meditatively
among green timber, through the grassy forest
towards a calm sea
and looking across to more of that great island
and the further topics.

1991

The Man with Night Sweats

I wake up cold, I who
Prospered through dreams of heat
Wake to their residue,
Sweat, and a clinging sheet.

My flesh was its own shield:
Where it was gashed, it healed.

I grew as I explored
The body I could trust
Even while I adored
The risk that made robust,

A world of wonders in
Each challenge to the skin.

I cannot but be sorry
The given shield was cracked
My mind reduced to hurry,
My flesh reduced and wrecked.

I have to change the bed,
But catch myself instead

Stopped upright where I am
Hugging my body to me
As if to shield it from
The pains that will go through me,

As if hands were enough
To hold an avalanche off.

1992

HORACE

iv.10 / To Ligurinus

Still cruel and still endowed with power to be so,

Gifted as you are with the gifts of Venus,

The moment is coming, when, suddenly, in the glass,

You see beginning the little signs of change,

Downy foreshadowing of the beard to come,

The locks that curl and wanton to the shoulders

All of a sudden looking a little different,

The cream-and-rose complexion beyond the beauty

Of freshest roses now not quite exactly

The way it had been just yesterday morning.

Then you will say, Alas for what I was

When I was younger than I am, Alas

That then I did not know what I know now;

Alas, that now I know what I did not know.

1997

Translated by David Ferry

Lines from the Testament

Solitude: you must be very strong
to love solitude; you have to have good legs
and uncommon resistance; you must avoid catching
colds, flu, sore throat; and you must not fear
thieves and murderers; if you have to walk
all afternoon or even all evening
you must do it with ease; there's no sitting down,
especially in winter, with wind striking the wet grass,
and damp mud-caked stone slabs among garbage;
there's no real consolation, none at all,
beyond having a whole day and night ahead of you
with absolutely no duties or limits.
Sex is a pretext. For however many the encounters
—and even in winter, through streets abandoned to the wind,
amid expanses of garbage against distant buildings,
there are many—they're only moments in the solitude;
the livelier and warmer the sweet body
that anoints with seed and then departs,
the colder and deathlier the beloved desert around you;
like a miraculous wind, it fills you with joy,
it, not the innocent smile or troubled arrogance
of the one who then goes away; he carries with him a youthfulness
awesomely young; and in this he's inhuman
because he leaves no traces, or, better, only one trace
that's always the same in all seasons.
A boy in his first loves
is nothing less than the world's fecundity.
It is the world that thus arrives with him, appearing, disappearing,
like a changing form. All things remain the same—
and you'll search half the city without finding him again;

the deed is done; its repetition is ritual. And
the solitude's still greater if a whole crowd
waits its turn: in fact the number of disappearances grows—
leaving is fleeing—and what follows weighs upon the present
like a duty, a sacrifice performed to the death wish.
Growing old, however, one begins to feel weary
especially at the moment when dinnertime is over
and for you nothing is changed; then you're near to screaming or weeping;
and that would be awesome if it wasn't precisely merely weariness
and perhaps a little hunger. Awesome, because that would mean
your desire for solitude could no longer be satisfied,
and if what isn't considered solitude is the true solitude,
the one you can't accept, what can you expect?
There's no lunch or dinner or satisfaction in the world
equal to an endless walk through the streets of the poor,
where you must be wretched and strong, brothers to the dogs.

1996

Translated by Norman MacAfee and Luciano Martinengo

JOSEPH BRODSKY

A Song

I wish you were here, dear,
I wish you were here.
I wish you sat on the sofa
and I sat near.
The handkerchief could be yours,
the tear could be mine, chin-bound.
Though it could be, of course,
the other way around.

I wish you were here, dear,
I wish you were here.
I wish we were in my car,
and you'd shift the gear.
We'd find ourselves elsewhere,
on an unknown shore.
Or else we'd repair
to where we've been before.

I wish you were here, dear,
I wish you were here.
I wish I knew no astronomy
when stars appear,
when the moon skims the water
that sighs and shifts in its slumber.
I wish it were still a quarter
to dial your number.

I wish you were here, dear,
in this hemisphere,
as I sit on the porch
sipping a beer.
It's evening, the sun is setting;
boys shout and gulls are crying.
What's the point of forgetting
if it's followed by dying?

1996

Arethusa

Ceres, happy again to have her daughter,
Returned to Arethusa, curious
To learn why she ran from home, and just how
She became a sacred fountain.

The pool grew calm as the goddess
Rose out of the depth.
She gathered up her green hair and from it
Wringing the heavy water began
The old story of how she was loved by a river.

"I was a nymph of Achaia.
None loved the woods,
And setting their hunting nets, as keenly as I did.
I was all action and energy,
And never thought of my looks.
Even so, my looks, yes, my beauty
Made others think of me.
The fame of my appearance burdened me.
The attractions
That all the other girls were sick to have
Sickened me, that I had them.
Because they attracted men, I thought them evil.

"There came a day
I had exhausted myself
In the Stymphalian Forest. The heat was frightening.
And my efforts, harrying the game,
Had doubled its effect on me.
I found a stream, deep but not too deep,

Quiet and clear—so clear,
Every grain of sand seemed magnified.
And so quiet, the broad clarity
Hardly dimpled.
The poplars and willows that drank at it
Were doubled in a flawless mirror.
I waded in—footsoles, ankles, knees.
Then stripped,
Hung my clothes on a willow
And plunged.
As I played there, churning the surface,
To and fro, diving to the bottom,
Swimming on my back, my side, my belly,
I felt a strange stir bulge in the current—
It scared me so badly
I scrambled up on to the bank.
A voice came after me:
'Why leave in such a hurry, Arethusa?'
It was Alpheus, in the swirl of his waters.
'Why leave in such a hurry?' he cried again.
I saw my clothes on the willow across the river.
I had come out on the wrong bank.
Naked as I was, I just ran—
That brought him after me
All the more eagerly—my nakedness
Though it was no invitation
Gave his assault no option.
I was like the dove in a panic
Dodging through trees when the hawk
Rides its slipstream
Tight as a magnet.

"The peak of Orchomenus went past,
And Psophis—
They were stepping stones
That my feet barely touched. Then Cyllene

And the knapped, flinty ridges
Of Maenalus, Erymanthus, and Elis—
The map rolled under me
As in a flight in a dream. He could not
Overtake me
But he could outlast me.
Over savannahs, mountains black with forest,
Pathless crags and gorges. But soon
The sun pressed on my back and I saw
That I ran in a long and leaping shadow—
The very shape of my terror—
And I heard the stones flying
From his striding feet, and his panting breath
That seemed to tug at my hair.

"In an agony of effort
I called to Diana:
'Help, or it's all over with me.
Remember how I carried your bow,
Your quiverful of arrows. Help me,
Help me, oh, help me.'

"The goddess heard and was stirred.
She brought up a dense mist
And hid me.
I smothered my gasping lungs. I tried
To muffle my heartbeat. And I froze.
I could hear the river-god, Alpheus,
Blindly casting about—
Twice he almost trod on me
Where I crouched under deep weeds.
'Arethusa!' he kept shouting, 'Arethusa!'
As if I would answer!
You can imagine what I was feeling—
What the lamb feels when the wolf's jaws
Are ripping the edge of the shed door.

Or what the hare feels
Peering through the wall of grass blades
When the circling hounds lift their noses.
But Alpheus persisted.
Circling the clump of mist, he could see clearly
My track that had gone in had not come out.
When I understood this
A sudden sweat chilled my whole body.
It streamed from me.
It welled from my hair. It puddled under my feet.
In the time it takes to tell you this
I had become a spring, a brisk stream,
A river, flowing away down the hillside.
But the river-god recognised me.
And he too dissolved his human shape,
Poured himself into his true nature
And mingled his current with my current.

"But Diana helped me again. She split earth open.
I dived into the gorge
And underground I came to Ortygia—
This land,
Which bears the name of my own beloved goddess,
Brought me back to light. That is my story."

1997

Version by Ted Hughes

Trying to Learn

I am trying to learn that this playful man who teases me is the same as that serious man talking money to me so seriously he does not even see me anymore and that patient man offering me advice in times of trouble and that angry man slamming the door as he leaves the house. I have often wanted the playful man to be more serious, and the serious man to be less serious, and the patient man to be more playful. As for the angry man, he is a stranger to me and I do not feel it is wrong to hate him. Now I am learning that if I say bitter words to the angry man as he leaves the house, I am at the same time wounding the others, the ones I do not want to wound, the playful man teasing, the serious man talking money, and the patient man offering advice. Yet I look at the patient man, for instance, whom I would want above all to protect from such bitter words as mine, and though I tell myself he is the same man as the others, I can only believe I said those words not to him, but to another, my enemy, who deserved all my anger.

1997

After Catullus

(For Thom Gunn on the occasion of his 60th birthday)

Heyho, loverboy
is that a radioactive isotope you've got
burning through your shirtfront
or are you just glad to see me?

                      Chump—
you couldn't bear it at her age
much less now.
Had you supposed the years made you pliant?
Look at yourself,

flesh hanging off you
same as the old fucks you take steam with
at the gym.
Better lay off the piss, buddyboy.

Think she doesn't notice?
She sees plenty.
Ask her girlfriends. Ask the hard-bellied punks
she has it off with in the dark.

Why don't you stop licking your nuts in the corner
like an injured tom.
And quit muttering.
You knew what you were up to

when you got into this.
All of your ex-sweethearts are arranged in a chorus,
each in a pinafore with dazzling florets,
laughing themselves sick.

1995

In Paris with You

Don't talk to me of love. I've had an earful
And I get tearful when I've downed a drink or two.
I'm one of your talking wounded.
I'm a hostage. I'm maroonded.
But I'm in Paris with you.

Yes I'm angry at the way I've been bamboozled
And resentful at the mess I've been through.
I admit I'm on the rebound
And I don't care where are *we* bound.
I'm in Paris with you.

>   Do you mind if we do *not* go to the Louvre,
>   If we say sod off to sodding Notre Dame,
>   If we skip the Champs Elysées
>   And remain here in this sleazy
>   Old hotel room
>   Doing this and that
>   To what and whom
>   Learning who you are,
>   Learning what I am.

Don't talk to me of love. Let's talk of Paris,
The little bit of Paris in our view.
There's that crack across the ceiling
And the hotel walls are peeling
And I'm in Paris with you.

Don't talk to me of love. Let's talk of Paris.
I'm in Paris with the slightest thing you do.
I'm in Paris with your eyes, your mouth,
I'm in Paris with ... all points south.
Am I embarrassing you?
I'm in Paris with you.

1994

Shirt

The back, the yoke, the yardage. Lapped seams,
The nearly invisible stitches along the collar
Turned in a sweatshop by Koreans or Malaysians

Gossiping over tea and noodles on their break
Or talking money or politics while one fitted
This armpiece with its overseam to the band

Of cuff I button at my wrist. The presser, the cutter,
The wringer, the mangle. The needle, the union,
The treadle, the bobbin. The code. The infamous blaze

At the Triangle Factory in nineteen-eleven.
One hundred and forty-six died in the flames
On the ninth floor, no hydrants, no fire escapes—

The witness in a building across the street
Who watched how a young man helped a girl to step
Up to the windowsill, then held her out

Away from the masonry wall and let her drop.
And then another. As if he were helping them up
To enter a streetcar, and not eternity.

A third before he dropped her put her arms
Around his neck and kissed him. Then he held
Her into space, and dropped her. Almost at once

He stepped to the sill himself, his jacket flared
And fluttered up from his shirt as he came down,
Air filling up the legs of his gray trousers—

Like Hart Crane's Bedlamite, "shrill shirt ballooning."
Wonderful how the pattern matches perfectly
Across the placket and over the twin bar-tacked

Corners of both pockets, like a strict rhyme
Or a major chord. Prints, plaids, checks,
Houndstooth, Tattersall, Madras. The clan tartans

Invented by mill-owners inspired by the hoax of Ossian,
To control their savage Scottish workers, tamed
By a fabricated heraldry: MacGregor,

Bailey, MacMartin. The kilt, devised for workers
To wear among the dusty clattering looms.
Weavers, carders, spinners. The loader,

The docker, the navvy. The planter, the picker, the sorter
Sweating at her machine in a litter of cotton
As slaves in calico headrags sweated in fields:

George Herbert, your descendant is a Black
Lady in South Carolina, her name is Irma
And she inspected my shirt. Its color and fit

And feel and its clean smell have satisfied
Both her and me. We have culled its cost and quality
Down to the buttons of simulated bone,

The buttonholes, the sizing, the facing, the characters
Printed in black on neckband and tail. The shape,
The label, the labor, the color, the shade. The shirt.

1996

FEDERICO GARCÍA LORCA

Absent Soul

The bull doesn't know you, nor the fig tree,
nor the horses, nor the ants of your own house.
The child doesn't know you, nor does the afternoon,
because you have died forever.

The face of the stone doesn't know you,
nor does the black satin in which your body breaks down.
Neither does the silenced memory of you know you
because you have died forever.

Autumn will come bringing sounds of conchs
and grapes of mist, and clustered hills,
but no one will want to look into your eyes
because you have died forever.

Because you have died forever,
like all the dead of the earth,
like all the dead who have been forgotten
on some heap of snuffed-out dogs.

No one knows you. No. But I sing of you.
I sing, for later on, of your profile and your grace.
The noble maturity of your understanding.
Your appetite for death and the taste of its mouth.
The sadness in your valiant gaiety.

There will not be born for a long time, if ever,
an Andalusian like him, so open, so bold in adventure.
I sing of his elegance in words that moan
and I remember a sad breeze in the olive grove.

1991

Translated by Christopher Maurer

Eclogue II

Corydon fell in love with a beautiful boy
Whose name was Alexis, the darling of his master.
So every day of the week he took himself
To the dense and gloomy shade of a beech-tree grove,
And flung out his hopeless ardor in artless verses:

"O Cruel Alexis, why are you deaf to my songs?
Have you no pity at all? Or don't you know
That Corydon's going to die for love of you?
Even the cows are seeking out the shade,
The little green lizards are hiding themselves in the bushes,
The laborers are worn out from the heat,
And Thestylis is pounding garlic and thyme,
Getting lunch ready, but under the burning sun
There's only my voice and the voice of the wailing locust.
Oh, wouldn't I have done better to put up with
The anger and haughty disdain of Amaryllis?
Or with Menalcas, swarthy though he is?
O fair Alexis, don't put too much trust
In your complexion. Remember that the blossoms
Of white privet fade and the darker blossoms
Of hyacinths are what the gatherers gather.
Perhaps you do not know, Alexis, who
It is you scorn: how many cows I have,
With all the milk they yield, summer and winter;
A thousand lambs, my lambs, pasture upon
These hills around; my voice is like the voice
Of Amphion on the slopes of Aracynthus,
Calling his herds. Nor is it that I'm bad-looking.
The other day when the wind was entirely still

And the sea was therefore like a mirror I saw
Myself in the mirror and said to myself that I,
If mirrors tell the truth, you being the judge,
Need never fear comparison with Daphnis.

"O Come and live with me in the countryside,
Among the humble farms. Together we
Will hunt the deer, and tend the little goats,
Compelling them along with willow wands.
Together singing we will mimic Pan,
Who was the first who taught how reeds could be
Bound together with wax to make a pipe.
Pan takes care with the shepherd and the sheep.
You oughtn't to mind if the reed bruises your lip;
Think how Amyntas practiced, learning to play.
Damoetas when he was dying bequeathed to me
This pipe I have, of seven hemlock stalks
Of different lengths. 'Now you're its master,' he said,
And foolish Amyntas was full of envy of me.
Besides the pipe I have two fawns I found
In a dangerous nearby valley, still so young
Their coats are speckled with white and eagerly
They feed at the udder of one of my ewes as if
They were really baby lambs; I've saved them for you;
Thestylis keeps telling me she wants them,
And maybe I'll give them to her, since it is clear
How little you think of the gifts I offer you.
O beautiful Alexis, come, see how
The Nymphs are bringing you baskets full of lilies,
See, the lovely Naiad makes a bouquet
Of palest violets and scarlet poppies for you,
Flower of fennel, narcissus blossoms also,
With yellow marigold and hyacinth,
And bound together with twine of cassia
And other fragrant herbs. And I myself
Will gather chestnuts as an offering,

And also downy peaches, and waxen plums,
Such as my Amaryllis used to love;
And I'll pluck laurel too, and the nearby myrtle,
The mingled perfume of them being so sweet.

"Corydon, you're a yokel. What makes you think
Alexis would care in the least about what you offer?
And as for gifts, would Iollas offer less?
Alas, alas, what have unhappy I
Been hoping for? In my distraction I
Have brought the sirocco down upon my flowers
And let the wild boar in to my crystal springs.
Ah, whom are you fleeing? A madman! Even the gods
Have lived in the woods, and Paris lived there too.
Let Pallas live in the city that she founded.
Let me dwell here lamenting in the forest.
The fierce lioness follows after the wolf,
The wolf pursues the goat, the wanton goat
Seeks out the flowering clover in the field,
And Corydon, Alexis, follows you.
Each creature is led by that which it most longs for.

"Look, here are the oxen come in from the fields,
Dragging the plow behind them, as the sun
Causes the shadows to lengthen and multiply,
And I still burn with love; love knows no limits.
Ah, Corydon, what madness has hold of you?
The vine on the leafy elm is only half-pruned—
Why not at least go about some needful task,
Binding the twigs together with pliant rushes.
There'll be another Alexis, if this one rejects you."

1999

Translated by David Ferry

"Do you still remember: falling stars,"

Do you still remember: falling stars,
how they leapt slantwise through the sky
like horses over suddenly held-out hurdles
of our wishes—did we have *so* many?—
for stars, innumerable, leapt everywhere;
almost every gaze upward became
wedded to the swift hazard of their play,
and our heart felt like a single thing
beneath that vast disintegration of their brilliance—
and was whole, as if it would survive them!

1996

Translated by Edward Snow

PHILIP LARKIN

Aubade

I work all day, and get half-drunk at night.
Waking at four to soundless dark, I stare.
In time the curtain-edges will grow light.
Till then I see what's really always there:
Unresting death, a whole day nearer now,
Making all thought impossible but how
And where and when I shall myself die.
Arid interrogation: yet the dread
Of dying, and being dead,
Flashes afresh to hold and horrify.

The mind blanks at the glare. Not in remorse
—The good not done, the love not given, time
Torn off unused—nor wretchedly because
An only life can take so long to climb
Clear of its wrong beginnings, and may never;
But at the total emptiness for ever,
The sure extinction that we travel to
And shall be lost in always. Not to be here,
Not to be anywhere,
And soon; nothing more terrible, nothing more true.

This is a special way of being afraid
No trick dispels. Religion used to try,
That vast moth-eaten musical brocade
Created to pretend we never die,
And specious stuff that says *No rational being*
Can fear a thing it will not feel, not seeing
That this is what we fear—no sight, no sound,
No touch or taste or smell, nothing to think with,

Nothing to love or link with,
The anaesthetic from which none come round.

And so it stays just on the edge of vision,
A small unfocused blur, a standing chill
That slows each impulse down to indecision.
Most things may never happen: this one will,
And realisation of it rages out
In furnace-fear when we are caught without
People or drink. Courage is no good:
It means not scaring others. Being brave
Lets no one off the grave.
Death is no different whined at than withstood.

Slowly light strengthens, and the room takes shape.
It stands plain as a wardrobe, what we know,
Have always known, know that we can't escape,
Yet can't accept. One side will have to go.
Meanwhile telephones crouch, getting ready to ring
In locked-up offices, and all the uncaring
Intricate rented world begins to rouse.
The sky is white as clay, with no sun.
Work has to be done.
Postmen like doctors go from house to house.

1989

——————

Odyssey XI, 40–90

Now the souls gathered, stirring out of Erebus,
brides and young men, and men grown old in pain,
and tender girls whose hearts were new to grief;
many were there, too, torn by brazen lanceheads,
battle-slain, bearing still their bloody gear.
From every side they came and sought the pit
with rustling cries; and I grew sick with fear.
But presently I gave command to my officers
to flay those sheep the bronze cut down, and make
burnt offerings of flesh to the gods below—
to sovereign Death, to pale Persephone.
Meanwhile I crouched with my drawn sword to keep
the surging phantoms from the bloody pit till
I should know the presence of Teiresias.

One shade came first—Elpenor, of our company,
who lay unburied still on the wide earth
as we had left him—dead in Kirke's hall, untouched,
unmourned, when other cares compelled us.
Now when I saw him there I wept for pity
and called out to him:

                                        "How is this, Elpenor,
how could you journey to the western gloom
swifter afoot than I in the black lugger?"
He sighed, and answered:

                                        "Son of great Laertes,
Odysseus, master mariner and soldier,
bad luck shadowed me, and no kindly power;

ignoble death I drank with so much wine.
I slept on Kirke's roof, then could not see
the long steep backward ladder, coming down,
and fell that height. My neck bone, buckled under,
snapped, and my spirit found this well of dark.
Now hear the grace I pray for, in the name
of those back in the world, not here—your wife
and father, he who gave you bread in childhood,
and your own child, your only son, Telemachus,
long ago left at home.

                                                    When you make sail

and put these lodgings of dim Death behind,
you will moor ship, I know, upon Aiaia Island;
there, O my lord, remember me, I pray,
do not abandon me unwept, unburied
to tempt the gods' wrath, while you sail for home;
but fire my corpse, and all the gear I had,
and build a cairn for me above the breakers—
an unknown sailor's mark for men to come.
Heap up the mound there, and implant upon it
the oar I pulled in life with my companions."

He ceased, and I replied:

                                                    "Unhappy spirit,

I promise you the barrow and the burial."

1998

Translated by Robert Fitzgerald

Milkweed and Monarch

—

As he knelt by the grave of his mother and father
the taste of dill, or tarragon—
he could barely tell one from the other—

filled his mouth. It seemed as if he might smother.
Why should he be stricken
with grief, not for his mother and father,

but a woman slinking from the fur of a sea-otter
in Portland, Maine, or, yes, Portland, Oregon—
he could barely tell one from the other—

and why should he now savour
the tang of her, her little pickled gherkin,
as he knelt by the grave of his mother and father?

—

He looked about. He remembered her palaver
on how both earth and sky would darken—
'You could barely tell one from the other'—

while the Monarch butterflies passed over
in their milkweed-hunger: 'A wing-beat, some reckon,
may trigger off the mother and father

of all storms, striking your Irish Cliffs of Moher
with the force of a hurricane.'
Then: 'Milkweed and Monarch "invented" each other.'

—

He looked about. Cow's-parsley in a samovar.
He'd mistaken his mother's name, 'Regan', for 'Anger':
as he knelt by the grave of his mother and father
he could barely tell one from the other.

1994

The Appalachian Book of the Dead

Sunday, September Sunday . . . Outdoors,
Like an early page from The Appalachian Book of the Dead,
Sunlight lavishes brilliance on every surface,
Doves settle, surreptitious angels, on tree limb and box branch,
A crow calls, deep in its own darkness,
Something like water ticks on
Just there, beyond the horizon, just there, steady clock . . .

Go in fear of abstractions . . .
                       Well, possibly. Meanwhile,
They *are* the strata our bodies rise through, the sere veins
Our skins rub off on.
For instance, whatever enlightenment there might be
Housels compassion and affection, those two tributaries
That river above our lives,
Whose waters we sense the sense of
                       late at night, and later still.

Uneasy, suburbanized,
I drift from the lawn chair to the back porch to the dwarf orchard
Testing the grass and border garden.
A stillness, as in the passageways of Paradise,
Bell jars the afternoon.
                Leaves, like *ex votos*, hang hard and shine
Under the endlessness of heaven.
Such skeletal altars, such vacant sanctuary.

It always amazes me

How landscape recalibrates the stations of the dead,

How what we see jacks up

      the odd quotient of what we don't see,

How God's breath reconstitutes our walking up and walking down.

First glimpse of autumn, stretched tight and snicked, a bad face lift,

Flicks in and flicks out,

     a virtual reality.

Time to begin the long division.

              1997

Sonnet of Intimacy

Farm afternoons, there's much too much blue air.
I go out sometimes, follow the pasture track,
Chewing a blade of sticky grass, chest bare,
In threadbare pajamas of three summers back,

To the little rivulets in the river-bed
For a drink of water, cold and musical,
And if I spot in the brush a glow of red,
A raspberry, spit its blood at the corral.

The smell of cow manure is delicious.
The cattle look at me unenviously
And when there comes a sudden stream and hiss

Accompanied by a look not unmalicious,
All of us, animals, unemotionally
Partake together of a pleasant piss.

1983

Translated by Elizabeth Bishop

DANTE ALIGHIERI

Inferno III, 67–108

Then, at the river—an old man in a boat:
  White-haired, as he drew closer shouting at us,
  "Woe to you, wicked souls! Give up the thought

Of Heaven! I come to ferry you across
  Into eternal dark on the opposite side,
  Into fire and ice! And you there—leave this place,

You living soul, stand clear of these who are dead!"
  And then, when he saw that I did not obey:
  "By other ports, in a lighter boat," he said,

"You will be brought to shore by another way."
  My master spoke then, "Charon, do not rage:
  Thus it is willed where everything may be

Simply if it is willed. Therefore, oblige,
  And ask no more." That silenced the grizzled jaws
  Of the gray ferryman of the livid marsh,

Who had red wheels of flame about his eyes.
  But at his words the forlorn and naked souls
  Were changing color, cursing the human race,

God and their parents. Teeth chattering in their skulls,
  They called curses on the seed, the place, the hour
  Of their own begetting and their birth. With wails

And tears they gathered on the evil shore
      That waits for all who don't fear God. There demon
      Charon beckons them, with his eyes of fire;

Crowded in a herd, they obey if he should summon,
      And he strikes at any laggards with his oar.
      As leaves in quick succession sail down in autumn

Until the bough beholds its entire store
      Fallen to the earth, so Adam's evil seed
      Swoop from the bank when each is called, as sure

As a trained falcon, to cross to the other side
      Of the dark water; and before one throng can land
      On the far shore, on this side new souls crowd.

"My son," said the gentle master, "here are joined
      The souls of all who die in the wrath of God,
      From every country, all of them eager to find

Their way across the water—for the goad
      Of Divine Justice spurs them so, their fear
      Is transmuted to desire. Souls who are good

Never pass this way; therefore, if you hear
      Charon complaining at your presence, consider
      What that means."

1994

Translated by Robert Pinsky

JAMES FENTON

Jerusalem

I

Stone cries to stone,
Heart to heart, heart to stone,
And the interrogation will not die
For there is no eternal city
And there is no pity
And there is nothing underneath the sky
No rainbow and no guarantee—
There is no covenant between your God and me.

II

It is superb in the air.
Suffering is everywhere
And each man wears his suffering like a skin.
My history is proud.
Mine is not allowed.
This is the cistern where all wars begin,
The laughter from the armoured car.
This is the man who won't believe you're what you are.

III

This is your fault.
This is a crusader vault.
The Brook of Kidron flows from Mea She'arim.
I will pray for you.
I will tell you what to do.
I'll stone you. I shall break your every limb.
Oh I am not afraid of you
But maybe I should fear the things you make me do.

IV

This is not Golgotha.

This is the Holy Sepulchre,

The Emperor Hadrian's temple to a love

Which he did not much share.

Golgotha could be anywhere.

Jerusalem itself is on the move.

It leaps and leaps from hill to hill

And as it makes its way it also makes its will.

V

The city was sacked.

Jordan was driven back.

The pious Christians burned the Jews alive.

This is a minaret.

I'm not finished yet.

We're waiting for reinforcements to arrive.

What was your mother's real name?

Would it be safe today to go to Bethlehem?

VI

This is the Garden Tomb.

No, *this* is the Garden Tomb.

I'm an Armenian. I am a Copt.

This is Utopia.

I came here from Ethiopia.

This hole is where the flying carpet dropped

The Prophet off to pray one night

And from here one hour later he resumed his flight.

VII

Who packed your bag?

I packed my bag.

Where was your uncle's mother's sister born?

Have you ever met an Arab?

Yes I am a scarab.

I am a worm. I am a thing of scorn.
      I cry Impure from street to street
And see my degradation in the eyes I meet.

VIII

      I am your enemy.
      This is Gethsemane.
The broken graves look to the Temple Mount.
      Tell me now, tell me when
      When shall we all rise again?
Shall I be first in the great body count?
      When shall the tribes be gathered in?
When, tell me, when shall the Last Things begin?

IX

      You are in error.
      This is terror.
This is your banishment. This land is mine.
      This is what you earn.
      This is the Law of No Return.
This is the sour dough, this the sweet wine.
      This is my history, this my race
And this unhappy man threw acid in my face.

X

      Stone cries to stone,
      Heart to heart, heart to stone.
These are the warrior archaeologists.
      This is us and that is them.
      This is Jerusalem.
These are the dying men with tattooed wrists.
      Do this and I'll destroy your home.
I have destroyed your home. You have destroyed my home.

1994

SEAMUS HEANEY

Bogland

for T. P. Flanagan

We have no prairies
To slice a big sun at evening—
Everywhere the eye concedes to
Encroaching horizon,

Is wooed into the cyclops' eye
Of a tarn. Our unfenced country
Is bog that keeps crusting
Between the sights of the sun.

They've taken the skeleton
Of the Great Irish Elk
Out of the peat, set it up,
An astounding crate full of air.

Butter sunk under
More than a hundred years
Was recovered salty and white.
The ground itself is kind, black butter

Melting and opening underfoot,
Missing its last definition
By millions of years.
They'll never dig coal here,

Only the waterlogged trunks
Of great firs, soft as pulp.
Our pioneers keep striking
Inwards and downwards,

Every layer they strip
Seems camped on before.
The bogholes might be Atlantic seepage.
The wet centre is bottomless.

1998

EUGENIO MONTALE

The Eel

The eel, siren
of cold seas, who leaves
the Baltic for our seas,
our estuaries, rivers, rising
deep beneath the downstream flood
from branch to branch, from twig to smaller twig,
ever more inward,
bent on the heart of rock,
infiltrating muddy
rills until one day
light glancing off the chestnuts
fires her flash
in stagnant pools,
in the ravines cascading down
the Apennine escarpments to Romagna;
eel, torch, whiplash,
arrow of Love on earth,
whom only our gullies
or desiccated Pyrenean brooks lead back
to Edens of generation;
green spirit seeking life
where only drought and desolation sting;
spark that says that everything begins
when everything seems charcoal,
buried stump;
brief iris,
twin to the one your lashes frame

and you set shining virginal among
the sons of men, sunk in your mire—
can you fail to see her as a sister?

1998

Translated by Jonathan Galassi

Your One Good Dress

should never be light. That kind of thing feels
like a hundred shiny-headed waifs backlit
and skeletal, approaching. Dripping and in
unison, murmuring, "We *are* you."

No. And the red dress (think about it,
redress) is all neckhole. The brown
is a big wet beard with, of course, a backslit.
You're only as sick as your secrets.

There is an argument for the dull-chic,
the dirty olive and the Cinderelly. But those
who exhort it are only part of the conspiracy:
"Shimmer, shmimmer," they'll say. "Lush, shmush."

Do not listen. It's a part of the anti-obvious
movement and it's sheer matricide. Ask your mum.
It would kill her if you were ewe gee el why.
And is it a crime to wonder, am I. In the dark a dare,

Am I now. You put on your Niña, your Pinta, your
Santa María. Make it simple to last your whole
life long. Make it black. Glassy or deep.
Your body is opium and you are its only true smoker.

This black dress is your one good dress.
Bury your children in it. Visit your pokey
hometown friends in it. Go missing for days.
Taking it off never matters. That just wears you down.

1999

THE
2000s

PAUL MULDOON

As

As naught gives way to aught
and oxhide gives way to chain mail
and byrnie gives way to battle-ax
and Cavalier gives way to Roundhead
and Cromwell Road gives way to the Connaught
and *I Am Curious (Yellow)* gives way to *I Am Curious (Blue)*
and barrelhouse gives way to Frank'N'Stein
and a pint of Shelley plain to a pint of India Pale Ale
I give way to you.

As bass gives way to baritone
and hammock gives way to hummock
and Hoboken gives way to Hackensack
and bread gives way to reed bed
and bald eagle gives way to Theobald Wolfe Tone
and the Undertones give way to Siouxsie Sioux
and DeLorean, John, gives way to Deloria, Vine,
and Pierced Nose to Big Stomach
I give way to you.

As vent gives way to Ventry
and the King of the World gives way to Finn MacCool
and phone gives way to fax
and send gives way to sned
and Dagenham gives way to Coventry
and Covenanter gives way to caribou
and the caribou gives way to the carbine
and Boulud's cackamamie to the cock-a-leekie of Boole
I give way to you.

As transhumance gives way to trance
and shaman gives way to Santa
and butcher's string gives way to vacuum pack
and the ineffable gives way to the unsaid
and pyx gives way to monstrance
and treasure aisle gives way to need-blind pew
and Calvin gives way to Calvin Klein
and Town and Country Mice to Hanta
I give way to you.

As Hopi gives way to Navaho
and rug gives way to rag
and *Pax Vobiscum* gives way to Tampax
and Tampa gives way to the water bed
and *The Water Babies* gives way to *Worstward Ho*
and crapper gives way to loo
and spruce gives way to pine
and the carpet of pine needles to the carpetbag
I give way to you.

As gombeen-man gives way to not-for-profit
and soft soap gives way to Lynn C. Doyle
and tick gives way to tack
and Balaam's Ass gives way to Mister Ed
and *Songs of Innocence* gives way to *The Prophet*
and single-prop Bar-B-Q gives way to twin-screw
and the Salt Lick gives way to the County Line
and "Mending Wall" gives way to "Build Soil"
I give way to you.

As your hummus gives way to your foul madams
and your coy mistress gives way to "The Flea"
and flax gives way to W. D. Flackes
and the living give way to the dead

and John Hume gives way to Gerry Adams
and Television gives way to U2
and Lake Constance gives way to the Rhine
and the Rhine to the Zuider Zee
I give way to you.

As dutch treat gives way to french leave
and spanish fly gives way to Viagra
and slick gives way to slack
and the local fuzz give way to the Feds
and Machiavelli gives way to make-believe
and *Howards End* gives way to *A Room with a View*
and Wordsworth gives way to "Woodbine
Willie" and stereo Nagra to quad Niagara
I give way to you.

As cathedral gives way to cavern
and cookie cutter gives way to cookie
and the rookies give way to the All-Blacks
and the shad give way to the smoke shed
and the roughshod give way to the Black Horse avern
that still rings true
despite that T being missing from its sign
where a little nook gives way to a little nookie
when I give way to you.

That *Nanook of the North* should give way to *Man of Aran*
as ling gives way to cod
and cod gives way to kayak
and Camp Moosilauke gives way to Club Med
and catamite gives way to catamaran
and catamaran to aluminum canoe
is symptomatic of a more general decline
whereby a cloud succumbs to a clod
and I give way to you.

For as Monet gives way to Juan Gris

and Juan Gris gives way to Joan Miró

and Metro-Goldwyn-Mayer gives way to Miramax

and the Volta gives way to Travolta, swinging the red-hot lead,

and *Saturday Night Fever* gives way to *Grease*

and the Greeks give way to you know who

and the Roman IX gives way to the Arabic 9

and nine gives way, as ever, to zero

I give way to you.

2002

GIUSEPPE UNGARETTI

Eternal

Between one flower plucked and the other given
the inexpressible nothing

2002

Translated by Andrew Frisardi

ELIZABETH BISHOP

Vague Poem (*Vaguely love poem*)

The trip west—
—I think I *dreamed* that trip.
They talked a lot of "Rose Rocks"
or maybe "Rock Roses"
—I'm not sure now, but someone tried to get me some.
(And two or three students had.)

She said she had some at her house.
They were by the back door, she said.
—A ramshackle house.
An Army house?—No, "a *Navy* house." Yes,
                        that far inland.
There was nothing by the back door but dirt
or that same dry monochrome, sepia straw I'd seen everywhere.
Oh she said the dog has carried them off.
(A big black dog, female, was dancing around us.)

Later, as we drank tea from mugs, she found one,
"a sort of one". "This one is just beginning. See—
you can see here, it's beginning to look like a rose.
It's—well, a crystal, crystals form–
I don't know any geology myself . . ."
(Neither did I.)
Faintly, I could make out—perhaps—in the dull,
rose-red lump of, apparently, soil,
a rose-like shape; faint glitters . . .   Yes, perhaps
there was a secret, powerful crystal at work inside.

I *almost* saw it: turning into a rose
without any of the intervening
roots, stem, buds, and so on; just
earth to rose and back again.
Crystalography and its laws:
something I   I once wanted badly to study,
until I learned that it would involve a lot of arithmetic, that is, mathematics.

Just now, when I saw you naked again,
I thought the same words: rose-rock; rock-rose . . .
Rose, trying, working to show itself,
forming, folding over,
unimaginable connections, unseen, shining edges.
Rose-rock, unformed, flesh beginning, crystal by crystal,
clear pink breasts and darker, crystalline nipples,
rose-rock, rose-quartz, roses, roses, roses,
exacting roses from the body,
and the even darker, accurate, rose of sex—

2006

Frederick Seidel

I live a life of laziness and luxury,
Like a hare without a bone who sleeps in a pâté.
I met a fellow who was so depressed
He never got dressed and never got undressed.

He lived a life of laziness and luxury.
He hid his life away in poetry,
Like a hare still running from a gun in a pâté.
He didn't talk much about himself because there wasn't much to say.

He found it was impossible to look or not to.
It will literally blind him but he's got to.
Her caterpillar with a groove
Waits for love

Between her legs. The crease
Is dripping grease.
He's blind—now he really is.
Can't you help him, gods!

Her light is white
Moonlight.
Or the Parthenon under the sun
Is the other one.

There are other examples but
A perfect example in his poetry is the what
Will save you factor.
The Jaws of Life cut the life crushed in the compactor

Out.

My life is a snout

Snuffling toward the truffle, life. Anyway!

It is a life of luxury. Don't put me out of my misery.

I am seeking more Jerusalem, not less.

And in the outtakes, after they pull my fingernails out, I confess:

I do love

The sky above.

2001

Crimson-Weave Carpet

Crimson-weave carpet,
silk reeled off select cocoons and boiled in clear water,
sun-bleached and steeped in dyes of crimdigo flower,

dyes turning thread crimson, indigo depths of crimson,
then woven to grace the Hall of Widespread Fragrance.

The Hall of Widespread Fragrance is a hundred feet long,
and the carpet's crimson weave will stretch end to end,

its iridescence soft and deep, its fragrance everywhere,
plush weave and mirage blossoms beyond all compare,

awaiting beautiful women who come to sing and dance,
gauze stockings and embroidered slippers sinking deep.

Even those carpets from T'ai-yüan seem stiff and rough,
and Ch'eng-tu rugs thin, their embroidered flowers cold:

they'll never compare to these, so warm and sumptuous
and sent each year from Hsüan-chou in the tenth month.

Hsüan-chou's grand prefect orders a new pattern woven,
saying they'll spare no effort on the emperor's behalf,

and then a hundred reverent men haul it into the palace,
the weave so thick and silk so lavish it can't be rolled up.

Can you fathom what it means, O prefect of Hsüan-chou:

for ten feet of carpet

a thousand taels of silk?

Floors don't feel the cold—people do. People need warmth.

No more floors dressed in clothes stolen from the people.

2008

Translated by David Hinton

Self-Portrait as the Red Princess

When the curtain rises,

       I appear in a red kimono, opening a paper umbrella.

Tucking my elbows into my waist,

       concealing my hands within my sleeves,

I circle the bare stage with tiny steps,

       holding my knees inward,

to create the impression I am small,

       because to be beautiful is to be small,

not young. I end in a dance of tears,

       placing my hand in a simple gesture

in front of my perfect oval face,

       indicating a woman's grief;

I am, after all, a woman,

       and not a man playing a woman.

Even with my mouth painted holly berry red

       and my waxed brows drawn higher,

there is nothing grotesque or cruel

       about my whitened, made-up face.

"The flower of verisimilitude," they call me—

       with my hair done up in a knot

of silver ornaments and lacquered wood

       and with my small melon seed face

filled with carnal love—

       though some nights sitting for hours

with my numb legs folded under me,

       pretending I have fallen out of love,

I cannot believe I am refining feminine beauty

       to a level unsurpassed in life.

Bathing with my lover,

       gazing at his firm stomach covered by hair,

pressing my burning face there,

                and, later, dashing to freedom in the black pines,

I see that I am veering toward destruction,

                instead of the unity of form and feeling;

I see a dimly shining instrument

                opening the soft meat of our throats.

Feeding and mating we share with the animals,

                but volition is ours alone.

Had I not followed a man to death,

                I think I would have died quietly,

as I had lived.

                             2003

Here

Here I am in the garden laughing
an old woman with heavy breasts
and a nicely mapped face

how did this happen
well that's who I wanted to be

at last   a woman
in the old style   sitting
stout thighs apart under
a big skirt   grandchild sliding
on   off my lap   a pleasant
summer perspiration

that's my old man across the yard
he's talking to the meter reader
he's telling him the world's sad story
how electricity is oil or uranium
and so forth   I tell my grandson
run over to your grandpa   ask him
to sit beside me for a minute   I
am suddenly exhausted by my desire
to kiss his sweet explaining lips

2000

PETRARCH

"My galley, loaded with forgetfulness,"

My galley, loaded with forgetfulness,
rolls through rough seas, at midnight, during winter,
aiming between Charybdis and sharp Scylla;
my lord, ah no, my foe, sits at the tiller;

each oar is wielded by quick, mad thought
that seems to scorn the storm and what it means;
an endless wind of moisture, of deep sighs,
of hopes and passions, rips the sail in half;

tears in a steady downpour, mists of hate,
are loosening and soaking all the ropes,
ropes made of ignorance, tangled up with error.

The two sweet stars I steer by are obscured;
reason and skill are dead amid the waves;
and I don't think I'll ever see the port.

2004

Translated by David Young

Riding Westward

Any sunset, look at him: standing there,
like between his legs there's a horse
somehow, on either side of it a saddlebag
of loss, a pack of sorrow, and him Kid
Compromise his very own shoot-'em-up
tilt to the brim of his hat self, smirk to match,
all-for-love-if-it's-gotta-come-to-that half
swagger,
       half unintentional, I think, sashay.
The silver spurs at his ankles where maybe
the wings would be, if the gods still existed,
catch the light, lose it, as he stands in place,
scraping the dirt with his boots: lines, circles
that stop short, shapes that mean nothing—
no bull, not like that, but scraping shyly, like
a man who's forgotten that part of himself,
keeps forgetting, because what the fuck?

As he takes his hat off; as he lifts his head
like if right now he could be any animal he'd
choose coyote; as all the usual sunset colors
break over his face,
       he starts up singing again,
same as every night, same song: loneliness
by starlight, miles to go, lay me down by
the cool, etc.—that kind of song, the kind
you'll have heard before, sure, somewhere,
but where *was* that,
       the singer turning this
and that way, as if watching the song itself

—the words to the song—leave him, as he
lets each go, the wind carrying most of it,
some of the words, falling, settling into
instead that larger darkness, where the smaller

darknesses that our lives were lie softly down.

                                                    2006

YUSEF KOMUNYAKAA

from "Autobiography of my Alter Ego"
"When my father was dying"

When my father was dying
                    he begged my mother
to forgive him, & she'd say,
                    Forgive you for what,
darling? He'd shake his head,
                        with a fat tear sliding down
the corner of his nose,
                    & he'd say, Honey,
I don't know.
            Between June & August,
two crows sat in the dogwood
                            outside their bedroom window,
& when their calling subsided,
                        my mother would say, Darling,
do you have the strength
                to forgive yourself?
Her question hung
            in the air—an old-old silence,
as if forgiveness
                was a luminous alchemy.
He'd look at me & say,
                Son, would you please
remind your mother,
                would you tell her what I did?
Big hero, with your Silver Star,
                    flesh of my flesh, your eyes
say you know all my secrets
                along this long road,

& the least a son can do

              is to help his father

nail his shadow to a pink dogwood.

2008

Crossroads

My body, now that we will not be traveling together much longer
I begin to feel a new tenderness toward you, very raw and unfamiliar,
like what I remember of love when I was young—

love that was so often foolish in its objectives
but never in its choices, its intensities.
Too much demanded in advance, too much that could not be promised—

My soul has been so fearful, so violent:
forgive its brutality.
As though it were that soul, my hand moves over you cautiously,

not wishing to give offense
but eager, finally, to achieve expression as substance:

it is not the earth I will miss,
it is you I will miss.

2009

Blood Dub

for Christine Hume

Crave your arrival, crave summer lines
to sow inside, Inspirer
crave beads from the tiny vial
crescents and pink tongue
crave vibrations while dining
the salt slide, crave stunning oil
and salivation trails, wet curls
crave tasting the plum drug
a purple pear on my ear
crave catlapping your lips
and the sun to swell as in the fable
of Jah's throb in a cherry aperture
and flood the folds

2004

Real Time

A merry-go-round reminds itself of flies,
listing dangerously in its element.
Thousands of years engrossed its sullen size.

In boiled wool and woolen lace, clockwise
our elders cinched a quad with ice o'ersprent
as merry-go-rounds bethought themselves of flies.

Glimpsed sharp in ragged dawn the old franchise
builds for us what they could have hardly meant.
Thousands of years engross its sullen size

that demon domestics haste to neutralize.
As in old flickers, laughs and colors blent
in a merry-go-round, doom themselves like flies—

though it's not urgent; there's time to entomologize.
We need only yawn, following the docent's
trail, and thousands of years engross our sullen size.

Age sags; little's left to elegize.
Waking from waltz-dream with time to repent
our merry-go-round bestirs itself, then flies.
Thousands of tears erode its sullen sides.

2002

Autumn Maneuver

I don't say: ah, yesterday. With worthless
summer money pocketed, we lie again
on the chaff of scorn, in time's autumn maneuver.
And the escape southward isn't feasible for us
as it is for the birds. In the evening,
trawlers and gondolas pass, and sometimes
a splinter of dream-filled marble pierces me
in the eye, where I am most vulnerable to beauty.

In the papers I read about the cold
and its effects, about fools and dead men,
about exiles, murderers and myriads
of ice floes, but little that comforts me.
Why should it be otherwise? In the face of the beggar
who comes at noon I slam the door, for we live in peacetime
and one can spare oneself such a sight, but not
the joyless dying of leaves in the rain.

Let's take a trip! Let's stroll under cypresses
or even under palms or in the orange groves
to see at reduced rates sunsets
that are beyond compare! Let us forget
the unanswered letters to yesterday!
Time works wonders. But if it arrives inconveniently
with the knocking of guilt: we're not at home.
In the heart's cellar, sleepless, I find myself again
on the chaff of scorn, in time's autumn maneuver.

2006

Translated by Peter Filkins

DON PATERSON

Parallax

the unbearable lightness of being no one
—SLAVOJ ŽIŽEK

The moon lay silent on the sea
as on a polished shelf
rolling out and rolling out
its white path to the self

But while I stood illumined
like a man in his own book
I knew I was encircled by
the blindspot of its look

Because the long pole of my gaze
was all that made it turn
I was the only thing on earth
the moon could not discern

At such unearthly distance
we are better overheard.
The moon was in my mouth. It said
A million eyes. One word

for Michael Longley

2010

"Passerby, these are words . . ."

Passerby, these are words. But instead of reading
I want you to listen: to this frail
Voice like that of letters eaten by grass.

Lend an ear, hear first of all the happy bee
Foraging in our almost rubbed-out names.
It flits between two sprays of leaves,
Carrying the sound of branches that are real
To those that filigree the unseen gold.

Then know an even fainter sound, and let it be
The endless murmuring of all our shades.
Their whisper rises from beneath the stones
To fuse into a single heat with that blind
Light you are as yet, who can still gaze.

Listen simply, if you will. Silence is a threshold
Where, unfelt, a twig breaks in your hand
As you try to disengage
A name upon a stone:

And so our absent names untangle your alarms.
And for you who move away, pensively,
Here becomes there without ceasing to be.

2006

Translated by Hoyt Rogers

MAHMOUD DARWISH

---

from "Eleven Planets at the End of the Andalusian Scene"

"On the Last Evening on this Earth"

On the last evening on this earth, we sever our days
from our trees, and count the ribs we will carry along
and the ribs we will leave behind, right here . . . on the last evening
we bid nothing farewell, we don't find the time to end who we are . . .
everything remains the same, the place exchanges our dreams
and exchanges its visitors. Suddenly we are incapable of satire
since the place is ready to host the dust . . . here on the last evening
we contemplate mountains surrounding clouds: a conquest and a
    counterconquest
and an ancient time handing over our door keys to the new time
so enter, you conquerors, our homes and drink our wine
out of our simple muwashah. We are the night when midnight comes, no
horseman carries the dawn from the ways of the final azaan . . .
our tea is hot and green so drink it, our pistachio fresh so eat it,
and our beds are cedar green, so surrender to sleepiness
after this long siege, sleep on our dreams' feathers,
the sheets are ready, the perfume by the door is ready, and the mirrors are
    many
for you to enter them so we can leave them entire. In a little while
we will search for what was our history around your history in the distant
    lands
and ask ourselves in the end: Was the Andalus
right here or over there? On earth . . . or in the poem?

2009

Translated by Fady Joudah

from *War Music*

"All in a moment on T'lespiax' note"

All in a moment on T'lespiax' note
10,000 javelins rose into the air
Catching the light but shadowing the ground
That lay between the enemies
    As Greece
Masks down, points down, in body-paint, in bronze
Beating their shields to trumpet drums and stunt-hoop tambourines
Advanced onto that ground
    While on T'lespiax' second note
Prince Hector's line of shield-fronts opened up
    —As Greece increased its pace—
To let their balaclavas led by Hux
(Who gave a farm the size of Texas for Cassandra)
Fender their scaffold pike-heads into Greece,
    As Greece:
    "Ave!"
    Now at a run
Came on through knee-deep dust beneath
Flight after flight from Teucer's up-ridge archers as:
    "Slope shields!"
    "Slope shields!"
The Trojan lords shout to their ranks,
And take the shock.

    Think of the moment when far from the land
    Molested by a mile-a-minute wind
    The ocean starts to roll, then rear, then roar
    Over itself in rank on rank of waves

Their sides so steep their smoky crests so high

300,000 plunging tons of aircraft carrier

Dare not sport its beam.

But Troy, afraid, yet more afraid

Lest any lord of theirs should notice any one of them

Flinching behind his mask

Has no alternative.

Just as those waves

Grown closer as they mount the continental shelf

Lift into breakers scoop the blue and then

Smother the glistening shingle

Such is the fury of the Greeks

That as the armies joined

No Trojan lord or less can hold his ground, and

Hapless as plane-crash bodies tossed ashore

Still belted in their seats

Are thrust down-slope.

2003

Beowulf, 2538–2591

"Then he drew himself up beside his shield."

Then he drew himself up beside his shield.
The fabled warrior in his warshirt and helmet
trusted in his own strength entirely
and went under the crag. No coward path.
Hard by the rock-face that hale veteran,
a good man who had gone repeatedly
into combat and danger and come through,
saw a stone arch and a gushing stream
that burst from the barrow, blazing and wafting
a deadly heat. It would be hard to survive
unscathed near the hoard, to hold firm
against the dragon in those flaming depths.
Then he gave a shout. The lord of the Geats
unburdened his breast and broke out
in a storm of anger. Under grey stone
his voice challenged and resounded clearly.
Hate was ignited. The hoard-guard recognized
a human voice, the time was over
for peace and parleying. Pouring forth
in a hot battle-fume, the breath of the monster
burst from the rock. There was a rumble under ground.
Down there in the barrow, Beowulf the warrior
lifted his shield: the outlandish thing
writhed and convulsed and vehemently
turned on the king, whose keen-edged sword,
an heirloom inherited by ancient right,
was already in his hand. Roused to a fury,
each antagonist struck terror in the other.
Unyielding, the lord of his people loomed

by his tall shield, sure of his ground,
while the serpent looped and unleashed itself.
Swaddled in flames, it came gliding and flexing
and racing towards its fate. Yet his shield defended
the renowned leader's life and limb
for a shorter time than he meant it to:
that final day was the first time
when Beowulf fought and fate denied him
glory in battle. So the king of the Geats
raised his hand and struck hard
at the enamelled scales, but scarcely cut through:
the blade flashed and slashed yet the blow
was far less powerful than the hard-pressed king
had need of at that moment. The mound-keeper
went into a spasm and spouted deadly flames:
when he felt the stroke, battle-fire
billowed and spewed. Beowulf was foiled
of a glorious victory. The glittering sword,
infallible before that day,
failed when he unsheathed it, as it never should have.
For the son of Ecgtheow, it was no easy thing
to have to give ground like that and go
unwillingly to inhabit another home
in a place beyond; so every man must yield
the leasehold of his days.

2000

Translated by Seamus Heaney

Retreat

The city abandoned; its citizens fled.
A paper chain hung on the wall left standing.
A single flip-flop graced the hardpacked floor.
The rest diminishes their loss: these were barracks,
and yesterday the men tried to blow a hole
through me as I squatted up the road
and took note of their grim frenzy,
like termites, no, more like tiny sailors
from a different time, when war came
over water and the battle arrived at a delay.
There was nothing to do but watch the enemy
grow from blot to galleon; colors nailed
to the mast. Like the bright orange flashing
we hung on our car's hood that said to the sky,
Don't bomb us, we are your friends.
These others, they had no friends in the sky.

2007

DURS GRÜNBEIN

Lament of a Legionnaire on Germanicus's Campaign to the Elbe River

There's nothing worse than this deadly retreat
following a battle, except the same retreat in prospect
weeks before . . .
Black as death the expression on the general's face,
the shambling, exhausted troops.
Behind the shields are the remnants of those unhurt,
footsore, running
with sweat. Incessant rain
has softened the tracks, the woods are one long ambush,
and the barbarians in packs, the wolves,
bite pieces out of our rear guard.
Whoever did not drown in the North Sea, far from home,
goes down in the swamps, as remote from the eternal city.
Overnight, morasses detain the whole legion,
by day it's rotten causeways, moldering ladders,
from whose rungs a man slips to his death
with fingers crushed. This land merely punctuates fog
like some archipelago at sea . . . Germania Magna,
where the forests are still integral and dense,
no tree bobs on the sea cut to a bank of oars—
or a blazing hulk. The futility of fighting
over provinces as vast as continents, and territories
that can only be defended by further wars.
In the depths of the forest there is no triumph, and no Latin order.
And when, aged by many years, you finally make it home,
it will be to see the German installed under your lintel,
and waving to you your wife's towheaded offspring.

2005

Translated by Michael Hofmann

Mu'allaqa

For Imru' Al-Qays

The elephant's trunk uncurling
From the lightning flashes
In the clouds was Marie Antoinette,
As usual trumpeting.
The greedy suction
Was her tornado vacuuming across the golden Kansas flatness.

Meanwhile, the count was talking to the swan.
The swan liked what he was saying and got
Right out of the pond.
Meanwhile, grown men in Afghanistan.
The count had fought in Algeria.
Meanwhile, neon in Tokyo.

Madame la Comtesse waved to us from the top step,
Waved to her count, their swan, their ornamental pond, *et moi.*
We were a towering cornucopia
Of autumn happiness
And *gourmandise* rotating counterclockwise,
Backwards toward the guillotine.

I kept a rainbow as a pet and grandly
Walked the rainbow on a leash.
I exercised it evenings together with the cheetah,
A Thorstein Veblen moment of conspicuous consumption:
A dapper dauphin in a T-shirt that said FRED
Parading with his pets decked out in T-shirts that said FRED'S.

I left my liver in the Cher.
I ate my heart out *en Berry*.
We drank and ate
France between the wars,
And every morning couldn't wait.
It felt sunshiny in the shadow of the château.

And when the rainbow leapt from there to here,
It landed twenty years away from the Cher.
The place it landed was the Persian Gulf.
It landed twinkling stardust where I'm standing in my life
With one-hump Marie Antoinette, my wife,
Who resembles that disarming camel yesterday.

In fact, the camel yesterday was smitten.
She left the other camels to come over.
You have a lovely liquid wraparound eye.
She stood there looking at me sideways.
They feed their racing camels caviar in Qatar.
The ruler of Dubai has said that he will try to buy Versailles.

A refrigerated ski slope, five stories high,
Lives improbably inside a downtown shopping mall in Dubai.
Arab men, wearing sneakers under their robes, hold hands.
Faceless black veils stop shopping to watch through the glass.
Seeing the skiers emphasizes the desert,
Like hearing far-off thunder at a picnic.

Both the word *thunder* and the word *picnic* are of course Arabic.
Indeed, Arabic was the language of French aristocrats
Before the Terror, bad body odor perfumed.
It is the language of the great Robert Frost poems,
Which have the suicide bomber's innocence
Walking safely past the checkpoint into the crowd.

They pay payola to Al Qaeda to stay away from Doha.
The emir was in his counting-house, counting out his oil and gas.
Another sunny Sunni day in the UAE!
A candidate for president
Who wants to manumit our oil-dependent nation
First has to get the message to every oily girl and boy

To just say no to up and down and in and out, labanotation
Of moaning oil rigs extracting oil joy.
My fellow Americans, I see a desert filled with derricks
Pumping up and down but never satisfied:
Obsessional hydraulics and Jimi Hendrix has hysterics.
I smash my guitar to bits onstage and that's all, folks!

It isn't.
I contemplate the end of the world. It isn't.
I have my croissant and café and the *Trib* and walk the rainbow
Around the block.
The young North African hipsters in the bitter *banlieues*
Contemplate the end of the world.

I contemplate the end of the world but in my case
It's not.
There are still things to buy.
I walk the rainbow in the dark.
The world is the kiosk where I get my *Herald Tribune*.
The world is my local café where my café au lait is quadroon.

I go to the strange little statue of Pierre Mendès-France
In the jardin du Luxembourg, in Paris, France.
I make a pilgrimage to it.
My quaint political saint and I visit.
The young North African hipsters in the bitter *banlieues*
Contemplate the end of the world, which isn't

The end of the world, though yes, quite true,
In Algeria and Afghanistan
Jihad is developing a dirty nuclear bomb
That smells like frangipani in flower
To keep Frangipani in power.
Ayatollah Frangipani has returned from his long exile in France

To annihilate vice.
I stomp the campfire out and saddle up my loyal *Mayflower*—
Who is swifter than a life is brief under the stars!
My prize four-wheel-drive with liquid wraparound eyes!
We ski the roller-coaster ocean's up and down dunes.
We reach land at last and step on Plymouth Rock.

2008

Bellosguardo

Oh how faint the twilight hubbub rising from
that stretch of landscape arching towards the hills—
the even trees along its sandbanks glow
for a moment, and talk together tritely;
how clearly this life finds a channel there
in a fine front of columns flanked by willows,
the wolf's great leaps through the gardens past the fountains
spouting so high the basins spill—this life
for everyone no longer possessed with our breath—
and how the sapphire last light is born again
for men who live down here; it is too sad
such peace can only enlighten us by glints,
as everything falls back with a rare flash
on steaming sidestreets, crossed by chimneys, shouts
from terraced gardens, shakings of the heart,
the long, high laughter of people on the roofs,
too sharply traced against the skyline, caught
between the wings and tail, massed branchings, cloud-
ends, passing, luminous, into the sky
before desire can stumble on the words.

2003

Version by Robert Lowell

This imitation of the first section of Montale's "Tempi di Bellosguardo" was found among
Lowell's papers after his death.

LAWRENCE JOSEPH

The Game Changed

The phantasmic imperium is set in a chronic
state of hypnotic fixity. I have absolutely
no idea what the fuck you're talking about
was his reply, and he wasn't laughing,
either, one of the most repellent human beings
I've ever known, his presence a gross and slippery
lie, a piece of chemically pure evil. A lawyer—
although the type's not exclusive to lawyers.
A lot of different minds touch, and have touched,
the blood money in the dummy account
in an offshore bank, washed clean, free to be
transferred into a hedge fund or a foreign
brokerage account, at least half a trillion
ending up in the United States, with more to come.
I believe I told you I'm a lawyer. Which has had
little or no effect on a certain respect
I have for occurrences that suggest laws
of necessity. I too am thinking of it
as a journey—the journey with conversations
otherwise known as the *Divina Commedia*
is how Osip Mandelstam characterized Dante's poem.
Lebanon? I hear the Maronite Patriarch
dares the Syrians to kill him, no word
from my grandfather's side of the family
in the Shouf. "There are circles here"—
to quote the professor of international
relations and anthropology—"Vietnam, Lebanon,
and Iraq . . . Hanoi, Beirut, and Baghdad."
The beggar in Rome is the beggar in Istanbul,
the blind beggar is playing saxophone,

his legs covered with a zebra-striped blanket,
the woman beside him holding an aluminum cup,
beside them, out of a shopping bag, the eyes
of a small, sick dog. I'm no pseudoaesthete.
It's a physical thing. An enthusiasm,
a transport. The melancholy is ancient.
The intent is to make a large, serious
portrait of my time. The sun on the market
near Bowling Green, something red, something
purple, bunches of roses and lilacs. A local
issue for those of us in the neighborhood.
Not to know what it is you're breathing
in a week when Black Hawk helicopters resume
patrolling the harbor. Two young men
blow themselves up attaching explosives
on the back of a cat. An insurgency:
commandos are employed, capital is manipulated
to secure the oil of the Asian Republics.
I was walking in the Forties when I saw it—
a billboard with a background of brilliant
blue sky, with writing on it in soft-edged,
irregularly spaced, airy-white letters
already drifting off into the air, as if they'd
been sky-written—"The World Really Does
Revolve Around You." The taxi driver rushes
to reach his family before the camp is closed—
"There is no way I will leave, there is no way—
they will have to kill us, and, even if
they kill every one of us, we won't leave." Sweat
dripping from her brow, she picks up the shattered,
charred bones. She works for the Commission
on Missing Persons. "First they kill them,"
she says, "then they burn them, then they cover them
with dead babies . . ." Neither impenetrable opacity
nor absolute transparency. I know what I'm after.
The entire poem is finished in my head. No,

I mean the entire poem. The color, the graphic
parts, the placement of solid bodies in space,
gradations of light and dark, the arrangements
of pictorial elements on a single plane
without a loss of depth. This habit of wishing—
as if one's mother and father lay in one's heart
and wished as they had always wished—that voice,
one of the great voices, worth listening to.
A continuity in which everything is transition.
To repeat it because it's worth repeating. Immanence—
an immanence and a happiness. Yes, exquisite—
an exquisite dream. The mind on fire
possessed by what is desired—the game changed.

2005

MICHAEL HOFMANN

My Father's House Has Many Mansions

Who could have said we belonged together,
my father and my self, out walking, our hands held
behind our backs in the way Goethe recommended?

Our heavy glances tipped us forward—the future,
a wedge of pavement with our shoes in it . . .
In your case, beige, stacked, echoing clogs;

and mine, the internationally scruffy tennis shoes—
seen but not heard—of the protest movement.
My mother shook her head at us from the window.

I was taller and faster but more considerate:
tense, overgrown, there on sufferance, I slowed down
and stooped for you. I wanted to share your life.

Live with you in your half-house in Ljubljana,
your second address: talk and read books;
meet your girlfriends, short-haired, dark, oral;

go shopping with cheap red money in the supermarket;
share the ants in the kitchen, the unfurnished rooms,
the fallible winter plumbing. Family was abasement

and obligation . . . The three steps to your door
were three steps to heaven. But there were only visits.
At a party for your students—my initiation!—

I ceremoniously downed a leather glass of *slivovica*.
But then nothing. I wanted your mixture of resentment
and pride in me expanded to the offer of equality.

Is the destination of paternity only advice . . . ?
In their ecstasy of growth, the bushes along the drive
scratch your bodywork, dislocate your wing-mirror.

Every year, the heraldic plum-tree in your garden
surprises you with its small, rotten fruit.

2009

My Mother's Lips

Until I asked her to please stop doing it and was astonished to find that she
not only could
but from the moment I asked her in fact would stop doing it, my mother, all
through my childhood,
when I was saying something to her, something important, would move her
lips as I was speaking
so that she seemed to be saying under her breath the very words I was saying
as I was saying them.

Or, even more disconcertingly—wildly so now that my puberty had
erupted—*before* I said them.
When I was smaller, I must just have assumed that she was omniscient. Why
not?
She knew everything else—when I was tired, or lying; she'd know I was ill
before I did.
I may even have thought—how could it not have come into my mind?—that
she *caused* what I said.

All she was really doing of course was mouthing my words a split second
after I said them myself,
but it wasn't until my own children were learning to talk that I really
understood how,
and understood, too, the edge of anxiety in it, the wanting to bring you
along out of the silence,
the compulsion to lift you again from those blank caverns of namelessness
we encase.

That was long afterward, though: where I was now was just wanting to get
her to stop,

and considering how I brooded and raged in those days, how quickly my
   teeth went on edge,
the restraint I approached her with seems remarkable, although her so
   unprotestingly,
readily taming a habit by then three children and a dozen years old was as
   much so.

It's endearing to watch us again in that long-ago dusk, facing each other, my
   mother and me.
I've just grown to her height, or just past it: there are our lips moving
   together,
now the unison suddenly breaks, I have to go on by myself, no maestro, no
   score to follow.
I wonder what finally made me take umbrage enough, or heart enough, to
   confront her?

It's not important. My cocoon at that age was already unwinding: the
   threads ravel and snarl.
When I find one again, it's that two o'clock in the morning, a grim hotel on
   a square,
the impenetrable maze of an endless city, when, really alone for the first
   time in my life,
I found myself leaning from the window, incanting in a tearing whisper
   what I thought were poems.

I'd love to know what I raved that night to the night, what those innocent
   dithyrambs were,
or to feel what so ecstatically drew me out of myself and beyond . . . Nothing
   is there, though,
only the solemn piazza beneath me, the riot of dim, tiled roofs and
   impassable alleys,
my desolate bed behind me, and my voice, hoarse, and the sweet, alien air
   against me like a kiss.

2006

Election Day

Though decked out in the Stars and Stripes,
the polling place was still a funeral home,
but then, ours was a precinct of funeral homes,
the way some neighborhoods are known
for their shoe stores or butcher shops.
On Election Day, the usually phantasmal aldermen
were out shaking hands, dressed in black
cashmere overcoats like proper mourners.
The air smelled of cigars and bars
and incense from the church whose doors
stood open as if at any moment
a coffin might come barging into traffic.
A cortege of dark Caddies lined the tow zones.
It might be a deceptive day with two-party weather:
one side of the street, Indian Summer,
December on the other, especially when wind
muscled the shadows that gathered as if the dead
were lurking—lost souls, spirits wandering
like drunks wondering where they'd parked
their cars, ghosts—most of them still voting.

2004

Reading Milosz

I read your poetry once more,
poems written by a rich man, knowing all,
and by a beggar, homeless,
an emigrant, alone.

You always wanted to go
beyond poetry, above it, soaring,
but also lower, to where our region
begins, modest and timid.

Sometimes your tone
transforms us for a moment,
we believe—truly—
that every day is sacred,

that poetry—how to put it?—
makes life rounder,
fuller, prouder, unashamed
of perfect formulation.

But evening arrives,
I lay my book aside,
and the city's ordinary din resumes—
somebody coughs, someone cries and curses.

2008

Translated by Clare Cavanagh

MARIE ÉTIENNE

from *King of a Hundred Horsemen*

"January. No one writes poetry any longer,
bric-a-brac in an old hardware store."

January. No one writes poetry any longer, bric-a-brac in an old hardware store.

What credence can be granted to words following each other, how can they still be thought possible?

Struggling against the even rhythm, one no longer holds one's hand to one's heart: the high old style till you're sick of it.

One walks one's words, one detaches them, spaces them, erases them.

One places them like a painter, as one would draw or embroider, cross-stitch.

One makes little piles, with no punctuation, "almost begging to write."

People talk to each other, talk.

The outside appears, but chronology, logic, are lacking.

Puddles remain.

"This is not a poem in this month of January."

This is not a novel unrolling its story, yet there, disguised by tears, a smile's incoherence.

Dialogues fade out, they are made of thought, repeated by an echo.

A silence is invoked, fingers on a windowpane, a step taken between tables.

Since one is benevolent, one says song and light.

2008

Translated by Marilyn Hacker

The Heart of Thomas Hardy

The heart of Thomas Hardy flew out of Stinsford churchyard
A little thumping fig, it rocketed over the elm trees.
Lighter than air it flew straight to where its Creator
Waited in golden nimbus, just as in eighteen sixty,
Hardman and son of Brum had depicted Him in the chancel.
Slowly out of the grass, slitting the mounds in the centre
Riving apart the roots, rose the new covered corpses
Tess and Jude and His Worship, various unmarried mothers,
Woodmen, cutters of turf, adulterers, church restorers,
Turning aside the stones thump on the upturned churchyard.
Soaring over the elm trees slower than Thomas Hardy,
Weighted down with a Conscience, now the first time fleshly
Taking form as a growth hung from the feet like a sponge-bag.
There, in the heart of the nimbus, twittered the heart of Hardy
There, on the edge of the nimbus, slowly revolved the corpses
Radiating around the twittering heart of Hardy,
Slowly started to turn in the light of their own Creator
Died away in the night as frost will blacken a dahlia.

2006

JAMES MCMICHAEL

Above the Red Deep-Water Clays

Capacity is both how
much a thing holds and how
much it can do. From a solid
magnetized and very hot core, the earth

suffers itself to be turned outside.
Closest to its heart are the deepest submarine
trenches and sinks. Its lava finds

clefts there in the old uplifted crust,
the ocean floor a scramble. Wrapping at depth huge

shield volcanoes, the North Atlantic

down- and upwells, its denser layers making
room behind them through the blue-green shortest
wavelengths of light. Inside the cubic
yards it levies,
league by league, respiring, budgeting its heat,

it hides its
samenesses of composition through and through.

For the normal water level,
an ideal
solitary wave is surplus. Any wave's
speed is what it is
only if reversing it would render it still.
Surfaces are almost without feature
at Sea Disturbance number one.

When the wind stretches them, their wrinkling gives it
more to hold on to. Three is
multiplying whitecaps.
Spray blows in well-marked streaks at six.
In the foam-spewed rolling swell that takes a

higher number,

small and medium
ships may be lost to view for a long time.
Waves are additive. Doming

up on the tidal bulge into a storm's
barometric low,
the distances between them widen
as from the Iceland-Faeroes massif

leeward for another
three hundred miles southeast

they build unblocked. Little

enough for them
the first outlying gabbro
islets and stacks. These are not yet *The British
Countryside in Pictures*, not yet the shoals
off Arran in the Firth of Clyde.

2006

The Pettichap's Nest

Well, in my many walks I rarely found
A place less likely for a bird to form
Its nest—close by the rut-gulled wagon road
And on the almost bare foot-trodden ground
With scarce a clump of grass to keep it warm,
And not a thistle spreads its spears abroad
Or prickly bush to shield it from harm's way,
And yet so snugly made that none may spy
It out save accident—and you and I
Had surely passed it in our walk to day
Had chance not led us by it—nay e'en now,
Had not the old bird heard us trampling by
And fluttered out, we had not seen it lie
Brown as the roadway side—small bits of hay
Plucked from the old propped-haystack's pleachy brow
And withered leaves make up its outward walls
That from the snub-oak dotterel yearly falls
And in the old hedge-bottom rot away.
Built like a oven with a little hole
Hard to discover that snug entrance wins,
Scarcely admitting e'en two fingers in,
And lined with feathers warm as silken stole
And soft as seats of down for painless ease
And full of eggs scarce bigger e'en than peas.
Here's one most delicate with spots as small
As dust—and of a faint and pinky red.
—Well, let them be and safety guard them well
For fear's rude paths around are thickly spread
And they are left to many dangers' ways
When green grasshoppers' jumps might break the shells,

While lowing oxen pass them morn and night
And restless sheep around them hourly stray
And no grass springs but hungry horses bite,
That trample past them twenty times a day.
Yet, like a miracle, in safety's lap
They still abide unhurt and out of sight.
—Stop, here's the bird—that woodman at the gap
Hath frit it from the hedge—'tis olive green—
Well, I declare, it is the pettichap!
No bigger than the wren and seldom seen:
I've often found their nests in chance's way
When I in pathless woods did idly roam,
But never did I dream until today
A spot like this would be her chosen home.

2003

A Lost Art

Vienna, 1805

There is no ceremony to stand on,
just walk in! No call to be dismayed:
it is not chaos you see in my shop,
but the leavings of creation; nothing
can do you any harm, and nothing is
so far along that you'll do harm to *it* . . .

Suppose you sit—just put that on the floor—
over here . . . Never mind, I can fix it:
legs are the least of my difficulties,
there! Welcome to the land of the missing,
where little is past recall. Or repair.
This? Oh, this is my *first* capybara,

I persuaded a chamberlain I know
at the Palace—whom you may know as well,
he's been up there for years, for *dynasties*:
Herr Pufendorf?—to let me have it back,
once I had pledged myself to substitute
a more convincing representative.

No, no, the eyes are set too high, and *green*!
a libel on the living article . . .
I keep it here, fallacious as it is,
to remind me, in a cautionary way,
that I can do (and have done) better work.
I have long since eclipsed such things, rising

from capybara to *homo capax*:
honest progress. A pity you cannot
confirm my boast; a word to Pufendorf,
not so long since, would have afforded you
the sight of my *magnum opus*, displayed
in the Imperial Museum—kept out

for years, just standing there in . . . state,
I have been told, in spite of protests from
the poor man's family. Not Pufendorf—
he has no family, to my knowledge!
"Poor man" refers to our black Angelo
Solyman, who was to be seen entire,

naked from head to heels, and all between,
the upshot of my labor and my skill . . .
It would have been no trick at all to do
a costumed figure, just the face and hands
set off by the white court dress, the gold braid,
the medals he invariably wore;

quite another matter to show the man's . . .
manhood, as my commission specified;
why, just to gain possession of the corpse
was a crime! Or would have been, if I'd
been caught: stolen at birth, stolen at death—
a slave's fate, for all the honors bestowed.

Then came the wife's compunction—she had been
widowed by a Flemish general and
married to Solyman in secret rite,
though in Saint Stephen's Cathedral. Yet
not even the Cardinal-Archbishop
could baffle the Emperor's plan. And I?

I did as I was ordered, did my best:
I allude to the *new* Emperor, of course,
not our late Joseph, who abhorred the sight
of stuffed animals of any species
(the entire Imperial family
suffered from this . . . susceptibility,

until Francis—in so many respects
the converse of his uncle). Now Francis,
Solyman safely dead, commanded me
to prepare, preserve and present him
as a perfect specimen *in all respects.*
He meant, of course, *in one*: I was to find

a way of representing what is held
to be the special virtue of black men,
although, however . . . outstanding in life,
our man's endowments were, most likely, dimmed
by being dead, revived in part and stuffed!
Moreover he had died quite civilly—

no evidence from the gibbet would grant
a hint of eventual scope to my art
nor any sculptor's manual of scale
suggest a means of reckoning how much
I might have to contend with. And I could
hardly ask the wronged widow for details!

An old cookery book delivered me:
by gently passing oil of cloves, it said,
over the affected body parts . . . Well,
even in the coldest larder, it seems,
an ox's member could be coaxed to life
or at least to life's dimensions, for a while.

And so it came about that Solyman—
born a prince in Pangusitlong, raised
a slave by robbers in Messina, sold
to one General Lobkowitz, by whom
he was bequeathed to Prince von Liechtenstein
who freed and later pensioned him for life—

a Mason, moreover, in Mozart's Lodge
(where both attended assiduously!)
who spoke German, Italian, English, French,
an excellent player of faro and chess,
observed in Frankfurt by the adolescent
Goethe at the Emperor's election—

this very Solyman you might have seen
for yourself in all his mortifying
splendor in the Museum, though of course
what I had studied to produce was more
of a demonstration piece—much visited
by our ladies, and some gentlemen too!—

than any emblem of human headway
in what civilization we may have—
something by way of a memorandum,
actually. No, I never visited:
I did the work, it is gone. Why torment
myself further? I know what I achieved.

I am told that after the bombardment
(though before Bonaparte entered the town)
the thing—my masterpiece!—was stolen
from its case by old Countess Zacharoff
and later vanished in the deplorable
looting of the Zacharoff residence . . .

2004

Loss Lieder

It's an icebox
missing freon,
elevator
that's kaput.
It's a danger
in the stashbox,
fast upon us
citigrade.
Lay your head
on radiators,
drive the needle
through the vein;
I'll be here when
you're no longer,
opal midnight
my refrain.
I'll sing it when
you're mentioned
if the cost is
not too great,
and if I haven't
met you coming
toward us
in the haze.

2009

MAUREEN N. MCLANE

Excursion Susan Sontag

Now Susan Sontag was famous
among certain people—you know
who I mean—urban informed culturally
literate East Coast people and some West
a few in Chicago in Europe and elsewhere although
Susan Sontag came from Arizona
which is remarkable
only if you hold certain prejudices
about Arizona which I do
having been there twice
and disliking it both times
not that this was Arizona's fault
it is majestic strange lunar orange desert
flat and then ravine-ridden but Phoenix
is heinous unless you have a certain
po-mo sensibility I associate with men
of a certain age and race and while
I share the supposed race I'm not a man although
there are men in Arizona but I forgot
to ask them what they thought
about the state or Susan Sontag
whose writings between 1964 and '67
are marvels of incisive thought and style
so much so that you have to wonder
what happened to America
what happened to Susan Sontag
who later published historical novels
in a realist mode when earlier she
championed the *nouveau roman*
oh where art thou where art thou Robbe-Grillet

and did her execution fail
her once-held prose ideals
oh is it our fate thus to lapse
if lapse it was and where is Sontag
to show us how to read Sontag
a professorial enthusiast
ringingly declared one Sunday Susan
"is always of the moment"
and thus we must conclude that in 1965
the new novel and criticism and sexy brains and France
were of the moment and now degraded realism
is of the moment as is "ethnic cleansing"
which Susan Sontag denounced indeed "put her life
on the line" (viz. enthusiast) producing Beckett
in Sarajevo she among the few
who spoke truly after 9/11 while torpor
overtook so many everyone waiting
for American Special Forces to "smoke"
Osama bin Laden "out of his hole"
on this matter Susan Sontag
held strong views e.g. about the president's
speech but she properly oriented us
to the club of men and one woman who advise him
since as she observed in an interview
on salon.com we are living in "a regency"
and we all know that regents are puppets
of their wily advisers cf. The Prince Regent
in England 1819 when aggrieved workers
gathered in Manchester and police agents
shot them tens hundreds dead maybe thousands
the papers covering up the massacre
whither media complicity is history now
and in England the people I met read several papers
expecting to compare and contrast each paper's
"take" on the news they didn't simply succumb
to the infantile American fantasy of media

"objectivity" the English and Irish
and Scots were like Burke unafraid
of prejudice they understood
you read through/with/against others'
prejudices and your own and thus Burke
against himself may be seen as an Enlightenment
theorist he supported the American Revolution
after all though he hysterically denounced
the French long before they guillotined anyone
o sweet Marie your fair chopped head
your luscious body the French pornographers
delighted in fucking tormenting reviling there
is a long affair between Enlightenment
philosophy and pornography as Cathleen Schine
explored in her spiky novel *Rameau's Niece*
as Sontag explored in a brilliant essay
of 1967 why are we so afraid
of porn there are many reasons the obvious
Freudian ones the "porn is rape" ones
the "protecting our children" ones the fear
of desire for the tabooed the "*jouissance*
of transgression" the world could blow up
any time but at the end
of the day it may all come down
to this our desire for knowledge
rips open the throat whole countries
have been seized with murder when threatened
with free inquiry not that those
who affiliate themselves self-righteously
with knowledge are not guilty of their own
simplifications because knowledge cuts
and opens wounds and distances
between lovers parents children citizens the world
feels different for example if you know
that somewhere people think god is dead
if the earth revolves around the sun

if you have stolen the gift of fire
if you know where your clitoris is and what
it can do and if you've seen Mapplethorpe's
whip stuck up his ass or his little devil's horns
perkily perched atop his mop of hair
why does he look so innocently rakish
is it because he's dead or that moment is or
is it my own perspective makes him so
not everything can be domesticated
or can it why did Proust avoid discussing
really discussing the mother now there is a crucial
evasion in an otherwise exhaustive
registration of the movements of consciousness
in society must old rockers and ACT UP veterans
and the Situationist International and Sontag all go
gentle into no that good that no that raging

2008

DON PATERSON

The Poetry

after Li Po

I found him wandering on the hill
one hot blue afternoon.
He looked as skinny as a nail,
as pale-skinned as the moon;

below the broad shade of his hat
his face was cut with rain.
Dear God, poor Du Fu, I thought:
It's the poetry again.

2010

THE
2010s

Forty Acres

to Barack Obama

Out of the turmoil emerges one emblem, an engraving—
a young Negro at dawn in straw hat and overalls,
an emblem of impossible prophecy: a crowd
dividing like the furrow which a mule has plowed,
parting for their president; a field of snow-flecked cotton
forty acres wide, of crows with predictable omens
that the young plowman ignores for his unforgotten
cotton-haired ancestors, while lined on one branch are a tense
court of bespectacled owls and, on the field's receding rim
is a gesticulating scarecrow stamping with rage at him
while the small plow continues on this lined page
beyond the moaning ground, the lynching tree, the tornado's black
    vengeance,
and the young plowman feels the change in his veins, heart, muscles,
    tendons,
till the field lies open like a flag as dawn's sure
light streaks the field and furrows wait for the sower.

2010

SINÉAD MORRISSEY
─────────────

The Coal Jetty

Twice a day,
    whether I'm lucky enough
        to catch it or not,

the sea slides out
    as far as it can go
        and the shore coughs up

its crockery: rocks,
    mussel banks, beach glass,
        the horizontal chimney stacks

of sewer pipes,
    crab shells, bike spokes.
        As though a floating house

fell out of the clouds
    as it passed
        the city limits,

Belfast bricks, the kind
    that also built the factories
        and the gasworks,

litter the beach.
    Most of the landing jetty
        for coal's been washed

away by storms; what stands—
    a section of platform
        with sky on either side—

is home now to guillemots
    and cormorants
        who call up

the ghosts of nineteenth-
    century hauliers
        with their blackened

beaks and wings.
    At the lowest ebb,
        even the scum at the rim

of the waves
    can't reach it.
        We've been down here

before, after dinner,
    picking our way
        over mudflats and jellyfish

to the five spiked
    hallways underneath,
        spanned like a viaduct.

There's the stink
    of rust and salt,
        of cooped-up

water just released
    to its wider element.
        What's left is dark and quiet—

barnacles, bladderwrack,
     brick—but book-ended
       by light,

as when Dorothy
     opens her dull
       cabin door

and what happens outside is Technicolor.

                                    2015

JOSHUA MEHIGAN

The Smokestack

The town had a smokestack.
It had a church spire.
The church was prettier,
but the smokestack was higher.

It was a lone ruined column,
a single snuffed taper,
a field gun fired at heaven,
a tube making vapor.

The smoke thinned the attention.
Its aspect kept transforming.
It could look like a cloud, or like
mosquitoes swarming.

The smokestack's bricks were yellow,
and its mouth twenty feet wide.
Its smoke was usually pale,
but there was a rust color on its side.

The smoke was yellow coral,
a bouquet of yellow roses,
a yellow beard, a yellow eye,
and sometimes runny noses.

Often it looked heavy
like junipers under snow.
At dawn it was limpidly pink
and shaped like an embryo.

It could look like Cuba
as seen from outer space.
It could look like a pedestal stone.
It could look like Jesus' face.

The busy residents
tended to ignore it,
though no one alive remembered
a time before it.

Sometimes it looked like ermine,
sometimes like elderflower.
Sometimes it looked like a Persian cat,
and sometimes like power.

It came before Lincoln Steffens.
It survived Eric Blair.
It was older than stop signs.
It would always be there,

resembling a tuxedo ruffle,
or an elephant head,
or a balled-up blanket
on a hospital bed.

It stopped three times a year,
but only for one day.
Once, in the '30s, it seemed to die.
Many families went away.

But it stayed dead a week,
and when it was resurrected,
the sky turned black, and then white,
as if a new pope were elected.

To labor it looked like a witness,
to management a snitch,
to both victim and perpetrator
it looked like getting rich.

At the Chamber of Commerce,
on a postcard of the square,
you'd find it in the background,
diminutive but there.

On cool summer evenings,
it billowed like azure silk.
On cold winter mornings,
it spread like spilled milk.

2014

Seawhere

America I am unnameable
Maybe you've never seen my skin my skin
Is brown but brown like   I might be Italian
Most often people think I'm Mexican

Once someone saw my double in Peru
She said *He had a noble soul*   I knew
Exactly what she meant   but smiled   Ameri-
ca now I might not have to smile   but this

Was 1995   and she meant well
I think   I am unnameable and so
I have no inner life no inner life
I recognize and so   I just don't know

Really what white , people are like inside
I know   better but worry the same goes for
Black people too   it was an accident I had
My childhood   black child raised by whites   and now

The problem isn't   that I don't see faces
Like mine it's that   I don't see inner lives
Like mine I mean the way   a person's inner
Life is expressed   partly by the public spaces

Created by their culture also   partly
By their behavior in those spaces I'm sub-
merged every day in the ocean of the inner
Lives of white people it's   white people mostly

To make my way through   you I have to borrow
An inner life   the way a scuba diver
Whose tank was empty might   borrow a mask
America   to make my way as Pharaoh

And Pharaoh's army made their way through the sea
Tell me where is the sea where   is the ocean
I cross to emigrate to you   I see
It nowhere   though it closes over me

2019

ANGE MLINKO

Gelsenkirchen

At some point they got off at Gelsenkirchen,
which is on the same train line as Hannover,
and while there, had their portraits taken.
That's all the sense I can make of this stopover
on their way to the coast, where the ships
were taking the faux Poles, the birchen people,
to whatever hospitable continent, on tips
circulating in the famine camps and steeple-
lands. Rotted frames, rusted nails, show their age:
the peeling backs, the glass glued now to them
like glass-topped coffins . . . the water damage
(my fault) that looks like ectoplasm.
Wherever they went they put icons side by side.
An embroidered linen cloth went over the top.
And so I place them, their calm looks borrowed
from those icons, and the photographer's shop,
"Im Lorenkamp," the historical clue I worry—
needlessly—since knowledge lives in imitation,
as in the train window, dark as boots and caraway,
they composed the mystery of salvation.

2017

The Small Dark Interior

The child seated in front,
her face close to the glass,
declared the pond frozen.
I was watching the shifting,
bronze grass and strayed
at her verdict. Her father
agreed too, but neatly distilled:
Glossed, honey, a bit iced—
but she was already
onto the drift-pocked, solitary
ducks across the bay's industrial
ruts, their stark white shapes
moving like phantoms in the marsh,
somewhere outside New Jersey.

I followed her pale head's
patient motion towards remnants
of what she saw—quiet now,
left hand at her jaw, the right dimmed
into her father's lap, a deeper silence.
Little Penseuse, I wanted to console:
you see the scene because you think it.
Then, instantly, the silver bullet
entered a tunnel and bound us
in the void, the hiss of steel a sea
straining homeward: *That is the land of lost content...*
But the child's reflection wiped
off the glass, and I panicked,
understanding what she meant
at the pond the autumnal

grass did not stir:
Instinct is older than the body.

As my eyes adjusted,
I found her, same position,
in the small dark, and decided
I am ready to forgive
my father his own flawed life.

2016

PETER COLE

Through the Slaughter

and Bialik

Sky—have mercy.
When flechettes fly
    forth from a shell,
    shot by a tank
        taking Ezekiel's
        chariot's name—

When their thin fins
invisibly whiz,
    whiffling the air
    like angels' wings—
        their metal feathers
        guiding them in—

When their hooks rip
through random flesh
    in a promise of land
    with its boring sun—
        Is it like the priests'
        release in Leviticus?

The male without blemish
and dashed blood?
    The limbs in pieces?
    The tents of meeting?
        The burnt offering?
        Does it hasten deliverance?

Or summon Presence?
Is its savor pleasant?
        As the rage unfurls
        in a storm of flame
                and the darts deploy
                in a shawl of pain,

does it soar like *justice*?
Contain a God?
        Expose a Source?
        What will is known?
                Does it touch *a throne*?
                Can we see a crown?

As the swarm scorches
the air with anger,
        and the torches of righteousness
        extend their reach—
                What power is power?
                Whose heart gives out?

When skin is *pierced*
to receive that flight,
        what light gets in?
        What's left of sin?
                What cause is served?
                What cry is heard?

When the blood of infants
and elders spurts
        across T-*shirts*
        does it figure *forever*?
                As it wreaks its change
                and seeks *revenge*

above the *abyss?*
Could Satan devise
    vengeance like this—
    war which is just . . .
        an art of darkness?
        Have mercy, skies.

Jerusalem, The Gaza War, 2014
2017

Over the Counties of Kings and Queens Came the Second Idea

After a long night swimming
In the dry dark of a book
I heard outside my window
A sound that changed my window.

Each of the planets unseen sang
As though in the grooves
Of a record I loved.
Saturn, Jupiter, Venus, Mars,

A scratch where the Earth
Where the Earth should be
Where the Earth should be
And is.

I stared out into the darkness
For some sign of the cold consoler,
That perched spinning
Night nurse who tends

To the sleeping sun
Destined to rise irresponsibly
Over the counties
Of Kings and Queens.

What are we during these
Archaic moments
Of mind-made Shangri-la
But bees trapped in amber,

Storyless and beheld,
By the amber god
Who makes it so
And the living god

Who undoes it?

2012

Almost Like the Blues

I saw some people starving
There was murder, there was rape
Their villages were burning
They were trying to escape
I couldn't meet their glances
I was staring at my shoes
It was acid, it was tragic
It was almost like the blues

I have to die a little
Between each murderous thought
And when I'm finished thinking
I have to die a lot
There's torture and there's killing
There's all my bad reviews
The war, the children missing
Lord, it's almost like the blues

I let my heart get frozen
To keep away the rot
My father says I'm chosen
My mother says I'm not
I listened to their story
Of the Gypsies and the Jews
It was good, it wasn't boring
It was almost like the blues

There is no G-d in Heaven
And there is no Hell below
So says the great professor
Of all there is to know
But I've had the invitation
That a sinner can't refuse
And it's almost like salvation
It's almost like the blues

2018

from *Time*

"I am a man 'planted beside streams of water,'"

I am a man "planted beside streams of water,"
but I'm not "blessed be the man."
The desert is calm all around me, but there's no peace in me.
Two sons I have, one still small,
and whenever I see a child crying
I want to make another one
as if I hadn't got it right
and wanted to start afresh.
And my father is dead, and God is only one, like me.
And the Hill of Evil Counsel sails into the night
all covered with antennae up to heaven.

I'm a man planted beside streams of water,
but I can only weep it,
and sweat it, and urinate it
and spill it from my wounds—
all this water.

2015

Translated by Ted Hughes

from *I Am the Beggar of the World*

"When sisters sit together, they always praise their brothers."

When sisters sit together, they always praise their brothers.
When brothers sit together, they sell their sisters to others.

2014

Translated by Eliza Griswold

Empathy

My love, I'm grateful tonight
Our listing bed isn't a raft
Precariously adrift
As we dodge the coast guard light,

And clasp hold of a girl and a boy.
I'm glad we didn't wake
Our kids in the thin hours, to take
Not a thing, not a favorite toy,

And didn't hand over our cash
To one of the smuggling rackets,
That we didn't buy cheap life jackets
No better than bright orange trash

And less buoyant. I'm glad that the dark
Above us is not deeply twinned
Beneath us, and moiled with wind,
And we don't scan the sky for a mark,

Any mark, that demarcates a shore
As the dinghy starts taking on water.
I'm glad that our six-year-old daughter,
Who can't swim, is a foot off the floor

In the bottom bunk, and our son
With his broken arm's high and dry,
That the ceiling is not seeping sky,
With our journey but hardly begun.

Empathy isn't generous,
It's selfish. It's not being nice
To say I would pay any price
Not to be those who'd die to be us.

2018

Black Figs

Because they tasted so damn good, I swore
    I'd never eat another one, but three seedy little hearts
beckoned tonight from a green leaf-shaped saucer,
    swollen with ripeness, ready to spill a gutty
sacrament on my tongue. Their skins too smooth
    to trust or believe. Shall I play Nat King Cole's
"Nature Boy" or Cassandra's "Death Letter"
    this Gypsy hour? I have a few words to steal
back the taste of earth. I know laughter can rip
    stitches, & deeds come undone in the middle of a dance.
Socrates talked himself into raising the cup to his lips
    to toast the avenging oracle, but I told the gods no
false kisses, they could keep their ambrosia & nectar,
    & let me live my days & nights. I nibble each globe,
each succulent bud down to its broken-off stem
    like a boy trying to make a candy bar last
the whole day, & laughter unlocks my throat
    when a light falls across Bleecker Street
against the ugly fire escape.

2011

"Very simple love that believes in words,"

Very simple love that believes in words,
since I cannot do what I want to do,
can neither hug nor kiss you,
my pleasure lies in my words
and when I can I speak to you of love.
So, sitting with a drink in front of me,
the place filled with people,
if your forehead quickly creases
in the heat of the moment I speak too loudly
and you never say don't be so loud,
let them think whatever they want
I draw closer melting with languor
and your eyes are so sweetly veiled
I don't reach for you, no, not even the softest touch
but in your body I feel I am swimming,
and the couch in the bar's lounge
when we get up looks like an unmade bed.

2013

Translated by J. D. McClatchy

They Were Not Kidding in
the Fourteenth Century

They were not kidding
when they said they were blinded
by a vision of love.

It was not just a manner
of speaking or feeling
though it's hard to say

how the dead
really felt harder
even than knowing the living.

You are so opaque
to me your brief moments
of apparent transparency

seem fraudulent windows
in a Brutalist structure
everyone admires.

The effort your life
requires exhausts me.
I am not kidding.

2014

Aubade

It's early, but I recognize this place.
I recognize the feeling, after an endless
Week of mornings in America, of returning
To the home one never really leaves,
Mired in its routines. I walk to what I try to
Tell myself is work, entering at the end of the day
The same room, like the man in *Dead of Night*—
The dinner, the DVD from Netflix,
The drink before I go to sleep and wake alone
In the dead of night like Philip Larkin
Groping through the dark at 4 a.m. to piss,
At home in the reality of growing old
Without ever growing up. I finally get up
An hour later, run, eat breakfast, read and write—
A man whose country is a state of mind,
A community of one preoccupied with time,
Leaving me with nothing much to do
But to write it off to experience—the experience
Of a rudimentary consciousness at 5 a.m.,
Aware of nothing but the drone
Of its own voice and a visual field
Composed of dogs and joggers in a park.

2018

Half-light

That crazy drunken night I
maneuvered you out into a field outside of

Coachella—I'd never seen a sky
so full of stars, as if the dirt of our lives

still were sprinkled with glistening
white shells from the ancient seabed

beneath us that receded long ago.
Parallel. We lay in parallel furrows.

—That suffocated, fearful
look on your face.

Jim, yesterday I heard your wife on the phone
tell me you died almost nine months ago.

Jim, now we cannot ever. Bitter
that we cannot ever have

the conversation that in
nature and alive we never had. Now not ever.

We have not spoken in years. I thought
perhaps at ninety or a hundred, two

broken-down old men, we wouldn't
give a damn, and find speech.

When I tell you that all the years we were
undergraduates I was madly in love with you

you say you
knew. I say I knew you

knew. You say
There was no place in nature we could meet.

You say this as if you need me to
admit something. *No place*

in nature, given our natures. Or is this
warning? I say what is happening now is

happening only because one of us is
dead. You laugh and say, Or both of us!

Our words
will be weirdly jolly.

That light I now envy
exists only on this page.

2017

A Foreshortened Journey

I found the stairs somewhat more difficult than I had expected and so I sat down, so to speak, in the middle of the journey. Because there was a large window opposite the railing, I was able to entertain myself with the little dramas and comedies of the street outside, though no one I knew passed by, no one, certainly, who could have assisted me. Nor were the stairs themselves in use, as far as I could see. You must get up, my lad, I told myself. Since this seemed suddenly impossible, I did the next best thing: I prepared to sleep, my head and arms on the stair above, my body crouched below. Sometime after this, a little girl appeared at the top of the staircase, holding the hand of an elderly woman. Grandmother, cried the little girl, there is a dead man on the staircase! We must let him sleep, said the grandmother. We must walk quietly by. He is at that point in life at which neither returning to the beginning nor advancing to the end seems bearable; therefore, he has decided to stop, here, in the midst of things, though this makes him an obstacle to others, such as ourselves. But we must not give up hope; in my own life, she continued, there was such a time, though that was long ago. And here, she let her granddaughter walk in front of her so they could pass me without disturbing me.

I would have liked to hear the whole of her story, since she seemed, as she passed by, a vigorous woman, ready to take pleasure in life, and at the same time forthright, without illusions. But soon their voices faded into whispers, or they were far away. Will we see him when we return, the child murmured. He will be long gone by then, said her grandmother, he will have finished climbing up or down, as the case may be. Then I will say goodbye now, said the little girl. And she knelt below me, chanting a prayer I recognized as the Hebrew prayer for the dead. Sir, she whispered, my grandmother tells me you are not dead, but I thought perhaps this would soothe you in your terrors, and I will not be here to sing it at the right time.

When you hear this again, she said, perhaps the words will be less intimidating, if you remember how you first heard them, in the voice of a little girl.

2014

The Setting of the Moon

As in the solitary night
over silvered countryside and water
where Zephyr gently breathes
and far-flung shadows
project a thousand lovely
insubstantial images and phantoms
onto still waves and branches,
hedges, hills, and farms;
reaching the horizon,
behind Apennine or Alp, or on the boundless
breast of the Tyrrhenian,
the moon descends, the world goes colorless,
shadows disappear, and one same darkness
falls on hill and valley.
Night is blind,
and singing with a mournful melody,
the carter on his way salutes
the last ray of the fleeting light
that led him on before.

So youth fades out,
so it leaves mortal life
behind. The shadows
and the shapes of glad illusions
flee, and distant hopes,
that prop our mortal
nature up, give way.
Life is forlorn, lightless.
Looking ahead, the wayward traveler
searches unavailingly

for goal or reason on the long
road he senses lies ahead,
and sees that man's home truly has become
alien to him, and he to it.

      Our miserable fate was judged
too glad and carefree up above
if youth, whose every happiness
is the product of a thousand pains,
should last for life;
the sentence that condemns
all living things to death too lenient
if first they were not given
a half-life far more cruel
than terrifying death itself.
The eternal gods invented—
great work of immortal minds—
the worst of all afflictions:
old age, in which desire is unfulfilled
and hope extinguished,
the fonts of pleasure withered,
pain ever greater, and with no more joy.

      You, hills and shores,
the splendor past that turned
the veil of night to silver in the west,
will not stay orphaned long,
for in the opposite
direction soon you'll see
the sky turn white again and dawn arise,
after which the sun,
flaming with potent fire
everywhere,
will bathe you and the heavenly fields
in floods of brilliance.
But mortal life, once lovely youth

has gone, is never dyed

by other light or other dawns again.

She remains a widow all the way.

And the Gods determined that the night

which hides our other times ends in the grave.

2010

Translated by Jonathan Galassi

"Love,"

Love,
the skeleton of a ship on the seabed
takes water as its flesh
and maybe schools of fish
as momentary sails. A single pearl
lost to a current
can become to it
a navigable star.

2016

The Embrace

As you lie beside me I edge closer,
taking sleep from your lips
as one wick draws flame from another.
And two night-lights are lit
as the flame takes and sleep passes
between us. But as it passes
the boiler in the basement shudders:
down there a fossil nature burns,
down in the depths prehistory's
sunken fermented peats blaze up
and slither through my radiator.
Wreathed in a dark halo of oil,
the bedroom is a close nest
heated by organic deposits,
by log pyres, leafmash, seething resins . . .
And we are the wicks, the two tongues
flickering on that single Paleozoic torch.

2010

Translated by Jamie McKendrick

The Ginger-Haired in Heaven

Sometimes only the ginger-haired in Heaven
can help me with my life. The flock of blondes
is sailing by so painlessly forgiven,
still blinking with love no one understands,

while the brunettes float thinking by the rushes
long after what they chose, long reconciled,
and here, the fair and sandy, all their wishes
half-granted them, half-wish them on a child.

Only the ginger-haired remember this, though:
this sulk and temper in the school of time,
this speckled hope and shyness at a window
as sunlight beats and blames and beckons. I'm

not coming out. They won't come out of Heaven,
or not until with auburn in the blood
two mortal tempers melt together. Even
then we might stay here if you said we could.

2011

Silver

I am the warper
caught in a weir
like a muscular tongue
against the teeth
or stuck with a spear
or reeled from the dark
to writhe on a hook
and make no sound
though sometimes heard
to whistle off-key
in a ruffled sound
or estuary

I am the warper
sniffing the air
and sliding across
rough wood and root
en route to pools
of Ira-waru
or branching streams
of Batasuna
though never at home
in the Pyrenees
preferring the deep
and rolling seas

I am the warper
pickled in brine
a cable wrapped
in gutta-percha

walloping north
as a spring unwinds
its subtle ribbon
beneath the keel
in a warp of murky
light and water
here and gone
a silver eel

2015

TOMAS TRANSTRÖMER

A Winter Night

The storm puts its mouth to the house
and blows to get a tone.
I toss and turn, my closed eyes
reading the storm's text.

The child's eyes grow wide in the dark
and the storm howls for him.
Both love the swinging lamps;
both are halfway towards speech.

The storm has the hands and wings of a child.
Far away, travellers run for cover.
The house feels its own constellation of nails
holding the walls together.

The night is calm in our rooms,
where the echoes of all footsteps rest
like sunken leaves in a pond,
but the night outside is wild.

A darker storm stands over the world.
It puts its mouth to our soul
and blows to get a tone. We are afraid
the storm will blow us empty.

2011

Translated by Robin Robertson

PAUL CELAN

"Answered"

Answered
by the transferred sparks
the fire-fragrance around
the pricket.

All
orbits are free.

Several earths
I lob to you while going blind—
the two
white ones you keep, one
in each hand.

The un-
buried, uncounted, up there,
the children,
are ready to jump—

You,
source-nightly, I
did not resemble:
you, joyous as
you now hover, are
impaled by the invisible, second,
standing firebrand.

2014

Translated by Pierre Joris

At Thomas Merton's Grave

We can never be with loss too long.
Behind the warped door that sticks,
the wood thrush calls to the monks,
pausing atop the stone crucifix,
singing: "I am marvelous alone!"
Thrash, thrash goes the hayfield:
rows of marrow and bone undone.
The horizon's flashing fastens tight,
sealing the blue hills with vermilion.
Moss dyes a squirrel's skull green.
The cemetery expands its borders—
little milky crosses grow like teeth.
How kind time is, altering space
so nothing stays wrong: and light,
more new light, always arrives.

2014

PABLO NERUDA

Ode to a Pair of Socks

Maru Mori brought me
a pair
of socks
that she knitted with her
shepherdess hands,
two socks soft
as rabbits.
I put my feet
into them
as into
two
cases
knitted
with threads of
twilight
and sheeps wool.

Wild socks,
my feet were
two wool
fish,
two big sharks
of ultramarine
crossed
by a golden braid,
two giant blackbirds,
two cannons:
my feet
were honored
in this way

by these
heavenly
socks.
They were
so beautiful
that for the first time
my feet seemed to me
unacceptable
like two decrepit
firemen, firemen
unworthy
of that
embroidered
fire,
of those shining
socks.

Anyway
I resisted
the sharp temptation
to save them
the way schoolboys
keep
lightning bugs,
the way scholars
collect
rare books,
I resisted
the mad impulse
to put them
in a golden
cage
and each day
to feed them birdseed
and the meat of a rosy melon.
Like explorers

in the forest
who give up the finest
young deer
to the roasting spit
and eat it
with regret,
I stretched out
my feet
and put on
the
lovely
socks
and then
my shoes.

And this is
the moral of my ode:
beauty is twice
beautiful
and goodness is doubly
good
when
it concerns two wool
socks
in winter.

2013

Translated by Mark Strand

Hive

All day we leave and arrive at the hive,
concelebrants. The hive is love,
what we serve, preserve, avowed in Latin murmurs
as we come and go, skydive, freighted
with light, to where we thrive, us, in time's hum,
on history's breath,

          industrious, identical . . .

there suck we,
alchemical, nectar-slurred, pollen-furred,
the world's mantra us, our blurry sound
along the thousand scented miles to the hive,
haven, where we unpack our foragers;
or heaven-stare, drone-eyed, for a queen's star;
or nurse or build in milky, waxy caves,
the hive, alive, us—how we behave.

2013

Dog Creek Mainline

Dog Creek: cat track and bird splay,
Spindrift and windfall; woodrot;
Odor of muscadine, the blue creep
Of kingsnake and copperhead;
Nightweed; frog spit and floating heart,
Backwash and snag pool: Dog Creek

Starts in the leaf reach and shoal run of the blood;
Starts in the falling light just back
Of the fingertips; starts
Forever in the black throat
You ask redemption of, in wants
You waken to, the odd door:

Its sky, old empty valise,
Stands open, departure in mind; its three streets,
Y-shaped and brown,
Go up the hills like a fever;
Its houses link and deploy
—This ointment, false flesh in another color.

*

Five cutouts, five silhouettes
Against the American twilight; the year
Is 1941; remembered names
—Rosendale, Perry and Smith—
Rise like dust in the deaf air;
The tops spin, the poison swells in the arm:

The trees in their jade death-suits,
The birds with their opal feet,
Shimmer and weave on the shoreline;
The moths, like forget-me-nots, blow
Up from the earth, their wet teeth
Breaking the dark, the raw grain;

The lake in its cradle hums
The old songs: out of its ooze, their heads
Like tomahawks, the turtles ascend
And settle back, leaving their chill breath
In blisters along the bank;
Locked in their wide drawer, the pike lie still as knives.

*

Hard freight. It's hard freight
From Ducktown to Copper Hill, from Six
To Piled High: Dog Creek is on this line,
Indigent spur; cross-tie by cross-tie it takes
You back, the red wind
Caught at your neck like a prize:

(The heart is a hieroglyph;
The fingers, like praying mantises, poise
Over what they have once loved;
The ear, cold cave, is an absence,
Tapping its own thin wires;
The eye turns in on itself.

The tongue is a white water.
In its slick ceremonies the light
Gathers, and is refracted, and moves
Outward, over the lips,
Over the dry skin of the world.
The tongue is a white water.)

2019

JAMES LASDUN

Blueberries

I'm talking to you old man.
Listen to me as you step inside this garden
to fill a breakfast bowl with blueberries
ripened on the bushes I'm planting now,
twenty years back from where you're standing.
It's strictly a long-term project—first year
pull off the blossoms before they open,
second year let them flower, watch the bees
bobbing in every bonnet,
but don't touch the fruit till year three,
and then only sample a handful or two . . .
Old man I'm doing this for you!
You know what they say about blueberries:
blood-cleansing, mood-lifting memory-boosters;
every bush a little fountain of youth
sparkling with flavonoids, anthocyanin . . .
I've spent all summer clearing brush,
sawing locust poles for the frames,
digging in mounds of pine needles, bales of peat moss—
I thought I'd do it while I still could.
You can do something for me in turn:
think about the things an old man should;
things I've shied away from, last things.
Care about them only *don't* care too
(you'll know better than I do what I mean
or what I couldn't say, but meant).
Reconcile, forgive, repent,
but don't go soft on me; keep the faith,
our infidels' implicit vow:
"Not the hereafter but the here and now . . ."

Weigh your heart against the feather of truth
as the Egyptians did, and purge its sin,
but for your own sake, not your soul's.
And since the only certain
eternity's the one that stretches backward,
look for it here inside this garden:
Blueray, Bluecrop, Bluetta, Hardy Blue;
little fat droplets of transubstantiate sky,
each in its yeast-misted wineskin, chilled in dew.
This was your labor, these are the fruits thereof.
Fill up your bowl old man and bring them in.

2015

BILL KNOTT

The Closet

(... after my mother's death)

Here not long enough after the hospital happened
I find her closet lying empty and stop my play
And go in and crane up at three blackwire hangers
Which quiver, airy, released. They appear to enjoy

Their new distance, cognizance born of the absence
Of anything else. The closet has been cleaned out
Full-flush as surgeries where the hangers could be
Amiable scalpels though they just as well would be

Themselves, in basements, glovelessly scraping uteri
But, here, pure, transfigured heavenward, they're
Birds, whose wingspans expand by excluding me. Their
Range is enlarged by loss. They'd leave buzzards

Measly as moths: and the hatshelf is even higher!
As the sky over a prairie, an undotted desert where
Nothing can swoop sudden, crumple in secret. I've fled
At ambush, tag, age: six, must I face this, can

I have my hide-and-seek hole back now please, the
Clothes, the thicket of shoes, where is it? Only
The hangers are at home here. Come heir to this
Rare element, fluent, their skeletal grace sings

Of the ease with which they let go the dress, slip,
Housecoat or blouse, so absolvingly. Free, they fly
Trim, triangular, augurs leapt ahead from some geometric
God who soars stripped (of flesh, it is said): catnip

To a brat placated by model airplane kits kids
My size lack motorskills for, I wind up glue-scabbed,
Pawing goo-goo fingernails, glaze skins fun to peer in as
Frost-i-glass doors . . . But the closet has no windows.

Opaque or sheer: I must shut my eyes, shrink within
To peep into this wall. Soliciting sleep I'll dream
Mother spilled and cold, unpillowed, the operating-
Table cracked to goad delivery: its stirrups slack,

Its forceps closed: by it I'll see mobs of obstetrical
Personnel kneel proud, congratulatory, cooing
And oohing and hold the dead infant up to the dead
Woman's face as if for approval, the prompted

Beholding, tears, a zoomshot kiss. White-masked
Doctors and nurses patting each other on the back,
Which is how in the Old West a hangman, if
He was good, could gauge the heft of his intended . . .

Awake, the hangers are sharper, knife-'n'-slice, I jump
Helplessly to catch them to twist them clear,
Mis-shape them whole, sail them across the small air
Space of the closet. I shall find room enough here

By excluding myself; by excluding myself, I'll grow.

2017

KAREN SOLIE

Affirmations

Has the past not pursued me with its face
and haven't I turned away?
Can a thing made once not be made again?

Hasn't the rider returned to her horse,
the dog to his master? Isn't this the lesson
of our popular literature?
And was the trash not collected
this morning, signalling no disruption
to the civic schedule?

Isn't the gesture, the act, inarguable?
And don't we live a parallel life in thought,
an attentiveness not unlike

a natural prayer of the mind and not-mind?
The shadow cast between them.
Where an unlight burns.

Won't nighttime reawaken and won't it be familiar?
Unequivocal through Carolinian forests
which have not wholly disappeared,
and equally among rows
of wrecked cars in the junkyards,
hoods open like a choir?

2015

Marina

Quis hic locus, quae regio, quae mundi plaga?

What seas what shores what grey rocks and what islands
What water lapping the bow
And scent of pine and the woodthrush singing through the fog
What images return
O my daughter.

Those who sharpen the tooth of the dog, meaning
Death
Those who glitter with the glory of the hummingbird, meaning
Death
Those who sit in the sty of contentment, meaning
Death
Those who suffer the ecstasy of the animals, meaning
Death

Are become unsubstantial, reduced by a wind,
A breath of pine, and the woodsong fog
By this grace dissolved in place

What is this face, less clear and clearer
The pulse in the arm, less strong and stronger—
Given or lent? more distant than stars and nearer than the eye

Whispers and small laughter between leaves and hurrying feet
Under sleep, where all the waters meet.

Bowsprit cracked with ice and paint cracked with heat.
I made this, I have forgotten
And remember.
The rigging weak and the canvas rotten
Between one June and another September.
Made this unknowing, half conscious, unknown, my own.
The garboard strake leaks, the seams need caulking.
This form, this face, this life
Living to live in a world of time beyond me; let me
Resign my life for this life, my speech for that unspoken,
The awakened, lips parted, the hope, the new ships.

What seas what shores what granite islands towards my timbers
And woodthrush calling through the fog
My daughter.

2018

CARL PHILLIPS

If You Will, I Will

To each his own urgency. I've spent this morning clearing
best as I can the strange pornography that last night's
storms made of the trees in the yard: oak and pear branches
everywhere; of the saplings, one broken, the other in need
of retying—its roots meanwhile, where the topsoil's gotten
washed away, left exposed to a spring that, not yet done settling
in, can't be trusted. I like a wreckage I can manage myself,
the chance it offers for that particular version of power
that comes from winnowing cleanly the lost from the still
salvageable, not erasing disorder exactly, but returning
order to a fair footing, at least, beside a wilderness I wouldn't
live without. I've got this friend—I guess you could call him that—
who worries I'll never stop courting recklessness—his
word for it—as a way of compensating for or maybe making
room, where there should

                                        be no room, for something torn
inside. Who can say if that's right? After a life of no signs
of it, he's found faith, and wants to know if I'm ready, finally,
to—as, again, he puts it—put my hand in the Lord's. For
the ancient Greeks—though others, too, must have thought this—
the gods were compelled most by rhythm, that's why ritual
was so important, the patterning of it, rhythm's lost
without pattern. I don't doubt that the gods—if that's
what you want to call whatever happens in this world, or
doesn't, or not as you hoped, or hoped for once it wouldn't—
seem as likely as any of us to be distracted by rhythm into
turning from one thing toward something else, but if what
comes in return is the gods' briefly full attention, though
magisterial at first, maybe—well, good luck dealing

with that. As when

intimacy seems nothing more, anymore, than
a form of letting what's been simple enough become difficult,
because now less far. Or as when, looking into a mirror,
I've looked closer still, and seen the rest that I'd missed earlier:
fierce regret, with its flames for fingers, hope as the not-so-
dark holdover from the dark before . . . Despite our differences,
we agree about most things, my friend and I, or let's say it
gets harder for me, as the years go by, to know for sure
he's wrong. It's like a game between us. He says my
moods are like the images any burst of starlings makes
against an open sky, before flying away. I say either no one's
listening, this late, or else anyone is. *You've changed*, he says,
getting slowly dressed again. *You don't know me*, I say, I say back.

2018

When I was beautiful

I was forgiven my raucous laughter.
Wedding guests

feasting like wasps
on soft-skinned fruits and sweetened wines,
even as a noise
more appallingly intimate

than thunder shocks some foreign air
into tiers of voile.
Leaves shuddering from trees;

the body harrowed of will.
My sister

was safe when I was beautiful.
I wore departure,

a jet's contrail, the initiate's reserve, a veil
of salt sowed over enemy orchards.

Danger drew me because I was beautiful.
I thought everyone heard

the voices I could, calling my name. The dead
needed me.
I've been so busy. So beautiful was I
my dress was the desert
where the ghost of moisture prowls
the rooftop sleepers, where dawn is kissed
without heat and cities gleam
like pearls.
Jealous morning. Who stole

my dreams. Which took from me
old men and families
strolling that unfamiliar promenade

as I calculated velocities,
   angles, routes

        of escape, while
the truck drove into us, exploding.
   I believed all the experts, who said
that in her own dreams
     the dreamer couldn't die.
Put away the pictures—they never show the face
in the mirror. The sun was in my eyes
    when I was beautiful.

           2013

Self-Portrait with Rifle

for Claire Malroux

Why do they lie down
when I shoot them?
Such open,
willing obedience
seems to come

from an inclination
to serve. I wish
I could control
myself better,
but I am not grown yet,

and the mystery
of death means
nothing to me.
Perhaps it is better
to be feared than loved.

The deer do not
seem to grieve
because of what
they have lost,
but instead

seem to just
lie down on
the forest floor—
after sauntering
like little cathedrals

with antler-spires—
something whole
in between
man and God,
cloaked with red

hair to the membranes
of their eyes.
How strange
not to remember
even the blows

to their heads
that made them sleep—
to be so absorbed
by experience
and then to forget.

2015

Self Help

The eye is the lamp of the body, so I tried
to make a world where all I ate was light. A butterfly
completes a similar labor in the summer
garden, beating its wings slowly like a healthy
person, the kind who runs for fun, could
run from an attacker, eats greens in the same
quantity as the salty meats the storytelling part
of us appears to favor. I couldn't decide
whether I wanted to stay alive or go
faster, they appeared to contradict each other, I tried
in all I did to eat light. I left the argument
about the difference between a slave and a servant
on the table, though I think what I think is that
consent to servitude is as much a fiction as a butterfly
having a nervous breakdown because of the beauty
of the lavender. The longer your hunger takes
to find a shape, the longer you can hold it. Consider the butterfly,
only at rest in the middle of consumption, but even
then preparing for departure, for disappearance,
closing in the middle of the landscape.
Trying to manage a world in which all you eat
is light is difficult. Labor, and the lungs should be like wings
of a butterfly beating, closing slowly, the moonlight
tensing the edge of each, almost lifting the edge of each
towards the middle distance. So all that I consume
can make me healthy, illuminate my throat
and the interstate of my digestive tract
with what a butterfly's been swimming in.

2019

ROBIN ROBERTSON

The Halving

(Royal Brompton Hospital, 1986)

General anaesthesia; a median sternotomy
achieved by sternal saw; the ribs
held aghast by retractor; the tubes
and cannulae drawing the blood
to the reservoir, and its bubbler;
the struggling aorta
cross-clamped, the heart
chilled and stopped and left to dry.
The incompetent bicuspid valve excised,
the new one—a carbon-coated disc, housed
expensively in a cage of tantalum—
is broken from its sterile pouch
then heavily implanted into the native heart,
bolstered, seated with sutures.
The aorta freed, the heart re-started.
The blood allowed back
after its time abroad
circulating in the machine.
The rib-spreader relaxed
and the plumbing removed, the breast-bone
lashed with sternal wires, the incision closed.

Four hours I'd been away: out of my body.
Made to die then jerked back to the world.
The distractions of delirium
came and went and then,
as the morphine drained, I was left with a split
chest that ground and grated on itself.

Over the pain, a blackness rose and swelled;
"pump-head" is what some call it
—debris from the bypass machine
migrating to the brain—but it felt
more interesting than that.
Halved and unhelmed,
I have been away, I said to the ceiling,
and now I am not myself.

2014

GOTTFRIED BENN

Little Aster

A drowned drayman was hoisted onto the slab.
Someone had jammed a lavender aster
between his teeth.
As I made the incision up from the chest
with the long blade
under the skin
to cut out tongue and palate,
I must have nudged it because it slipped
into the brain lying adjacent.
I packed it into the thoracic cavity
with the excelsior
when he was sewn up.
Drink your fill in your vase!
Rest easy,
little aster!

2013

Translated by Michael Hofmann

Buried Alive

It's always in the past, that orgasm.
Always in the present, that double.
Always in the future, that panic.

Always in my chest digs that claw.
Always in my boredom waves that hand.
Always in my sleep there's war.

Always in my dealings, no deal at all.
Always in my signature, that old fury.
Always the same error, with a new likeness.

Always in my leaps there's that limit.
Always on my lips, a wax seal.
Always in my no, that trauma.

Always in my love, sudden night.
Always in myself, my enemy.
And always in my always, the same absence.

2015

Translated by Richard Zenith

Vanitas Varietatum

Now and then I ask myself
if this world really is the world
and if these women among the park's paths
really are the mothers.
Why do they stroke a gloved hand
along the backs of their faithful dogs?
why do scottish children
spy on someone from behind the trees,
student or soldier
who opens a paper bag now
full of nougats or sugar candy?
October is red and comes down the mountains
from house to house
and from chestnut tree to chestnut tree
it presses against the women's cloaks
it caresses the flag on the bungalow
the very day the soldiers, the *bersaglieri*,
enter Trieste again.
Therefore everything is soft under the trees
near the mothers and their orange cloaks
the world, the world and every pain of love
does any other pain exist?
they are there, outside the gates: thus the Furies
and their endless works.

But these aren't the mothers
I'm sure of it, these are the waiting deer.

2012

Translated by Charles Wright

To a Giraffe

If it is unpermissible, in fact fatal
to be personal and undesirable

to be literal—detrimental as well
if the eye is not innocent—does it mean that

one can live only on top leaves that are small
reachable only by a beast that is tall?—

of which the giraffe is the best example—
the unconversational animal.

When plagued by the psychological
a creature can be unbearable

that could have been irresistible;
or to be exact exceptional

since less conversational
than some emotionally-tied-in-knots animal.

     After all
consolations of the metaphysical
can be profound. In Homer, existence

is flawed; transcendence, conditional;
the journey from sin to redemption, perpetual.

2017

A Scattering

I expect you've seen the footage: elephants,
finding the bones of one of their own kind
dropped by the wayside, picked clean by scavengers
and the sun, then untidily left there,
    decide to do something about it.

But what, exactly? They can't, of course,
reassemble the old elephant magnificence;
they can't even make a tidier heap. But they can
hook up bones with their trunks and chuck them
    this way and that way. So they do.

And their scattering has an air
of deliberate ritual, ancient and necessary.
Their great size, too, makes them the very
embodiment of grief, while the play of their trunks
    lends sprezzatura.

Elephants puzzling out
the anagram of their own anatomy,
elephants at their abstracted lamentations—
may their spirit guide me as I place
    my own sad thoughts in new, hopeful arrangements.

2017

Thick Description

I cut lines of ink as I read through the night.
I imagine the margins on pages are slim wings
between plankton and stars. I find what I need
in far sources. I make them intimate,

I make them mine with the speed of light.

He was seventeen, just a man, still a boy and ready to die.
A true sacrifice, a living encounter—
                                This father has paid
the sum of a daughter's dowry for his son to be consecrated
with a rod through his cheeks and tongue. The boy's face,
his mouth pierced and gaping, hangs on the page, helpless.

His clove-jelly eyes float and metamorphose into my mother's
eyes, eyes I can't possibly remember without images like his—
images forbidden, seized and smuggled into my life.
I can make anything mean what I need to find.

The stolen scrap, the plosive glance saturated in
longing is not looking at me: I am looking at *it*.
Every description is thick with a will to revivify—
reclaim, renounce, rename what is sought.

Blind hunger drives when I read. *A scream, the echo of*
a scream, hangs over that Nova Scotian village . . . and bit
by bit a village I've never seen swells into me. The ovoid
mouth of my mother's life, its slivering silence exists

in that scream—*unheard, in memory*. She came alive
forever—*not loud, just alive forever* redeemed from her never
with no speech. A noun transformed to modify
action revived her, returned her to me.

The words as they lay may refuse to say what you need.
Drop to your knees. Crawl beneath the overhanging,
the dangling down. Stroke the described,
from underneath. It reeks of the atavistic

to live. It survives by swallowing.

2016

ALEKSANDR KUSHNER

"Here's what I envy: Prussian blue,"

Here's what I envy: Prussian blue,
Deep cobalt blue—the sea reaches
In a slender band from behind
The mountains and it streams like smoke;
Having gone back through my life,
I envy red ochre, verdurous earth;
Leave a tube of the color "P. Veronese"
Beside me here on the table,
Arrange the near, out-spilling foreground
So that its leaves brocade the sun,
And the English would understand me,
The Japanese would take me up.

Oh brilliant yellow, give me heart,
Carmine and madder lake, serve me here
In place of the word, which requires translation,
And still winds up in the dark.

The artist is at a loss
To explain: come up and look.
He's used to creeping through ribgrass
As prose stylists do through *Madame Bovary*.
What I envy him are his gestures, his exclamations,
His bellowing, the glister of zinc white,
Not his opinion—some remark
As to the honey tone of the banister.

I too would brighten my palette,
But the old earthly horror restrains me,
The passerby on his artificial limb,
The neighbor's sick child.
I could sit out on the grass
In a sailor-stripe vest and straw hat,
Sipping now and again from my flask,
And disown the murky word.
For I do envy ultramarine, and how
The laundry hangs on the line . . .

I will never ever leave you,
black and white word of mine!

2015

Translated by Carol Ueland and Robert Carnevale

CHARLES BERNSTEIN

A Defence of Poetry

For Brian McHale

My problem with deploying a term liek
nonelen
in these cases is acutually similar to
your
cirtique of the term ideopigical
unamlsing as a too-broad unanuajce
interprestive proacdeure.
You say too musch lie a steamroller when
we need dental (I;d say jeweller's)
tools.
(I thin youy misinterpret the natuer of
some of the political claims go; not
themaic
interpretatiomn of evey
evey detail in every peim
but an oeitnetation towatd a kind of
texutal practice
that you prefer to call "nknsense" but
for *poltical* purpses I prepfer to call
ideological!
, say Hupty Dumpty)
Taht is, nonesene see,msm to reduce a
vareity of fieefernt
prosdodic, thematic and discusrive
enactcemnts into a zeroo degree of
sense. What we have is a vareity of
valences. Nin-sene.sense is too binary
andoppostioin, too much oall or nithing

account with ninesense seeming by its
very meaing to equl no sense at all. We
have preshpas a blurrig of sense, whih
means not relying on convnetionally
methods of *conveying* sense but whih may
aloow for dar greater sense-smakinh than
specisi9usforms of doinat disoucrse that
makes no sense at all by irute of thier
hyperconventionality (Bush's speeches,
calssically). Indeed you say that
nonsenese shed leds on its "antithesis"
sense making: but teally the antithsisi
of these poems you call nonselnse is not
sense-making itslef but perhps, in some
cases, the simulation of sense-making:
decitfullness, manifpulation, the
media-ization of language, etc.
I don't agree with Stewart that "the
more exptreme the disontinuities . . . the
more nonsisincial": I hear sense
beginning to made in this sinstances.
Te probelm though is the definaitonof
sense. What you mean by nomsense is
soething like a-rational, but ratio (and
this does back to Blake not to meanion
the pre-Socaratics) DOES NOT EQUAL
sense! This realtioes to the sort of
oscillation udnertood as rhytmic or
prosidci, that I disusccio in Artiofice.
Crucialy, the duck/rabitt exmaple is one
of the ambiguity of *aspects* and clearly
not a bprobelm of noneselnse: tjere are
two competing, completely sensible,
readings, not even any blurring; the
issue is context-depednece)otr
apsrevcyt blindness as Witegenstein

Nonesesen is too static. Deosnt't
Prdunne even say int e eoem "sense occurs
"at the contre-coup:: in the process of
oscillatio itself.
b6y the waylines 9–10 are based on an
aphorism by Karl Kraus: *the closer we
look at a word the greater the distance
from which it stares back.*

2010

Poem in a Style Which Is Not Mine

to thee, Baudelaire

Near a holly tree through whose leaves a town could be seen, Don Juan, Rothschild, Faust, and a painter were conversing.

"I have amassed an enormous fortune," Rothschild said, "and, since it has brought me no pleasure, I continue to accumulate, hoping to find again the joy my first million brought me."

"I have continued to seek love in the midst of misfortunes," said Don Juan. "To be loved and not to love is torture, but I continued to seek love in the hope of finding the emotion of first love again."

"When I found the secret that made me famous," said the painter, "I sought other secrets to occupy my mind; for these I was refused the fame that first one had brought me, and I return to my old formula despite the disgust it inspires in me."

"I gave up knowledge for happiness," said Faust, "but I come back to knowledge, despite the fact that my methods are out of date, because there is no happiness except in seeking."

Beside them was a young girl with a crown of artificial ivy who said:

"I am bored; I am too beautiful!"

And God spoke behind the holly tree:

"I know the universe; I am bored."

2014

Translated by John Ashbery

CHRISTIAN WIMAN

From a Window

Incurable and unbelieving
in any truth but the truth of grieving,

I saw a tree inside a tree
rise kaleidoscopically

as if the leaves had livelier ghosts.
I pressed my face as close

to the pane as I could get
to watch that fitful, fluent spirit

that seemed a single being undefined
or countless beings of one mind

haul its strange cohesion
beyond the limits of my vision

over the house heavenwards.
Of course I knew those leaves were birds.

Of course that old tree stood
exactly as it had and would

(but why should it seem fuller now?)
and though a man's mind might endow

even a tree with some excess
of life to which a man seems witness,

that life is not the life of men.
And that is where the joy came in.

2010

THE

2020s

On My Seventy-Eighth

There will be just two at
table tonight,
though to accommodate all those who have
so mattered
and still so matter in my life, the table will be
very long:
though empty. I say to you, *Jaya*
shoma khalee!
Your place is empty! Your place at my table
is saved
for you. I tried to construct in my soul
your necessary
grave (because you were dead/because you were
flawed/preoccupied,
concentrated on your soul, too often you were
cruel—) but
as I shoveled dirt onto your body, the dirt refused,
soon, to
cling. Those who torment because you know you
loved them
refuse to remain buried. *Is anything ever forgotten,*
actually forgiven?
Shovel in hand, I saw how little I had
known you.
Tonight, I abjure the wisdom, the illusion of
forgetting. Come,
give up silence. Intolerable the fiction
the rest

is silence. To the dead, to the living:
your place
is empty.

2021

EUGENIO MONTALE

The Arno at Rovezzano

The great rivers are the image of time,
cruel and impersonal. Seen from a bridge
they say their inexorable nothingness.
Only the hesitant bend of a swampy
clump of reeds, of mirrors flashing
in thick brush and stonecrop can make clear
that water thinks itself like us
before it becomes whirlpool and destruction.
So much time has passed yet nothing's happened
since I sang you "*Tu che fai l'addormentata*"
on the phone, guffawing madly.
Your house was a flash of lightning from the train,
leaning over the Arno like the Judas tree
that tried to protect it. Maybe it's still there,
or it's a ruin. Infested with insects,
you said, uninhabitable.
It offers us other comforts now,
other discomforts.

2024

Translated by Jonathan Galassi

AUGUST KLEINZAHLER

Snow Approaching on the Hudson

Passenger ferries emerge from the mist
    river and sky, seamless, as one—
        watered ink on silk

then disappear again, crossing back over
    to the other shore, the World of Forms—
        as-if-there-were, as-if-there-were-not

The buildings on the far shore ghostly
    afloat, cinched by cloud about their waists—
        rendered in the *boneless* manner

Cloud need not resemble water
    water need not resemble cloud—
        breath on glass

The giant HD plasma screen atop Chelsea Piers
    flashing red and green—
        stamped seal in a Sesshu broken ink scroll

A tug pushes the garbage scow, left to right, toward the sea
    passing in and out of the Void—
        vaporizing gray, temporal to timeless

Clouds wait, brooding for snow
    and hang heavily over the earth—
        Ch'ien Wei-Yen

Bustle of traffic in the sky, here, as well, on the shore below
    obliterated—
        empty silk

The wind invisible
    spume blown horizontal in the ferry's wake—
        wind atmosphere, river silk

2020

Ephphatha

Jesus Christ, my dusty socialist,
"There's enough sun for everyone," you state,
your crown chipped like a front tooth
after a bar fight. Behind you a red curtain.
You're — well, hard to tell *what* you are . . .
The hymnals boxed in tubs in the lady chapel.
Closed seven months, we open St. Mark's
in Jackson Heights, Queens, New York City.
Queens, the unnoticed and mocked borough.
Can anything good come out of Nazareth?
Late August, sun on the slate, and God

is it hot! Vestry, you interview me.
Who am I? The wardens, Henry and Jorge,
unlock the safe with the broken tumbler
in the sacristy. The priest's office window
rusted shut. Adjusting surgical masks
over our noses to unmuffle our voices,
we are a wedge —

You move with us, you always have,
you and your circumspect circumference.
The streets jounce with languages and carts
with mango slices in zip-locks, all of it
personal, none of it personal. The 7 train
slides on its rails. It's a pandemic. Single king,
you beckon from the buckling blue glass
donated by someone everyone has forgotten.
We sweat and sit with no AC.

My white guayabera sticks
to my pocked back like a sealed envelope.

2024

Sing a Darkness

Slowly the fog did what fog does, eventually: it lifted, the way
veils tend to at some point in epic
      verse so that the hero can
see the divinity at work constantly behind
all things mortal, or that's
      the idea, anyway, I'm not saying I do or don't
believe that, I'm not even sure that belief can change
any of it, at least in terms of the facts of how,
      moment by moment, any life unfurls, we can
call it fate or call it just what happened, what
happens, while we're busy trying to *describe*
      or *explain* what happens,
how a mimosa tree caught growing close beside a house
gets described as "hugging the house,"
      for example, as if an impulse to find affection everywhere
made us have to put it there,
a spell against indifference,
      as if that were the worst thing—
is it?
Isn't it?
      The fog lifted.
It was early spring, still.
The dogwood brandished those pollen-laden buds
      that precede a flowering. History. What survives, or doesn't.
How the healthiest huddled, as much at least
as was possible, more closely together,
      to give the sick more room. How they mostly all died, all the same.

I was nowhere I'd ever been before.

Nothing mattered.

I practiced standing as still as I could, for as long as I could.

2022

HANNAH SULLIVAN

---

from "Repeat Until Time"
"When things are patternless,
their fascination's stronger."

When things are patternless, their fascination's stronger.
Failed form is hectic with loveliness, and compels us longer.

The horse chestnut gets on tediously with its leaves,
Provides spiked toys, diets middle-aged in winter,
Gets low-carb skeletal, squash lean, only to
Have another go with the old Cool Whip come spring.

The oak tree is absurd as new parents amazed
That a baby's nails need cutting, dead keratin: so slick
So dull, that eternal kernel rigmarole,
The bee-sucked flower, the pig-shat nut,
From which, what junky miracle, new oak trees grow?

The pollarded tree is subtler, its season a fungal autumn.
The branches that were husbanded will never grow clean.
But stunted they stay, an old woman's cobbled knees,
Thick legs beneath a butterball skirt, a green flare,
Her skirts lifted high as she dances to wedding music.

Rolled-up sleeves around each cut-back head
End in slender new sprouts,
Crooked forearms shot from the bark.

You think of Alabama at noon,
A quiet clapboard church,
White shirts rolled up, dust motes
Antsy on the windows, in the heat,
An uncertain hosanna.

It is hard to say if there is progress in history.

2020

Even Homer Nods

You can be a mother who knows a god.
And you can ask him for magic armor,
A shield the width of Saturn's widest rings,
Some helmet in the new or ancient style,
Fill your arms with defenses for your child,
Take the peacock feather you've been offered
And plant it in that helmet's crown, or keep it
For yourself to use as a pen, note this
Was the only option you were offered,
Stylist or witness, witness with stylus,
So that you'd circle down the drain with death,
Mourning in either silence or sound bites,
Surrounded by silence and sound bites, life
Like this having been polished to shine
In the normal ways things shine these days,
A dull lull, the type of insufficient glare
We used to call out on sight as useless
Glow but now in new darkness we feel a need
For, a consolation of presence,
As when my mother passed me the soft shield,
The breastplate like rice paper, the helmet
Bright as pyrite can be, we already
Knew that this was part of the old cycle,
That I would die soon, without a weapon,
And she'd live on, and we'd do this again
And again and again, without ever
Knowing we were the weapon ourselves,
Stronger than steel, story, and hydrogen,

Here in America, where we wonder,
Still, after everything that's happened, why
Anyone bothers to read the classics.

2020

Venice, Florida

The clouds went on each afternoon—
bodybuilding to a rippling mass,
flat-topped, or with bedhead;
from a puffball, picayune,
they did something to the grass
fluorescing on the watershed.

It rained so hard all summer long,
every field was canalized
by overflow or turned into lagoon.
The fountain jets burped a song
of bullfrogs poolside, bull's-eyed,
prelude to a honeymoon.

Electricity's appendages, like
butterfly filaments, alit on things,
charging the soil with nitrogen,
so you'd run, as though Nike
grabbed your ankles by their wings,
and you were an Olympian.

On one of these afternoons,
you met your tennis coach,
storms needling the atmosphere,
clouds like hydroponic blooms,
roots whitening on approach.
You should have shown more fear,

hitting balls that greenly blazed
in the hyacinthine climate;

like statuary, your torso flexed
on tiptoe, your arm upraised
to execute a serve, until the wet
match fizzled out. (There's a text

that warns boys of hubris!)
Then things would clear.
A dragonfly would gondolier
through the misted air and seem
to offer a golden balance beam
to the showboating iris.

A calmness floods the aftermath.
This is the secret of summer eves,
when ultramarine bands the earth,
twin to the blue hour in the north.
Not snowfields but grass and leaves
dusk milks blue for all they're worth.

2022

Psalm

NoOne kneads us again of earth and clay,
noOne conjures our dust.
Noone.

Praised be thou, NoOne.
For your sake we
want to flower.
Toward
you.

2020

Translated by Pierre Joris

Cum Clave

The night sky on the vaulted
Ceiling of the Sistine Chapel
Was hacked off star by gold star
For Michelangelo to make the
World from scratch.

I think I remember a serene birth.
My pink body & the blue pulsing rope
Cut by a masked man.
My mother's long thighs
Painted in blood & water as
My father's blue eyes looked first
Into the universe of my mouth.

I can't see the stop-motion
Lions hunting in the Lascaux cave.
They are being saved
From my breath;
They are being preserved
For future bodies to destroy.
But I want to breathe on those
Lions & watch them run.

It's my skin, my sweat & my breath
That destroys Michelangelo's ceiling too.
You locked my mouth closed with your
Finger key in your Porsche in Rome
Until I nodded, *Yes, you own me.*
Every time I remember you, I alter you.

Michelangelo made his God a man
& gave his Moses horns.
It's the wet of my body &
My breath that destroys you too.

2021

ELIZA GRISWOLD

Goodbye, Mullah Omar

Wormwood grows on the one-eyed Mullah's grave.
The Talib boys fight blindly on believing he's alive.
—ANONYMOUS

Charlie says when Afghan men get together,
the number of eyes is always odd.

A generation has outdated wounds.
No longer cool, or relevant, the Taliban

can't muster the fear they used to.
The duffers stalk the graveyard and the chowk,

finger their hennaed beards. They cultivate cartoon.
Once, a deaf-mute pressed her thumb to chin

to warn me they were coming,
the universal symbol, Fear the Beard.

There's ancient precedent for their love
of the fore-flattened image.

In medieval painting, failure is a prayer.
To render perspective less precisely

indicates humility.
The bowed head knows its flaws.

The land belongs to ISIS now.
No one settles for an eye;

how quaint, how Deuteronomy.
The depiction that matters

is inflicting suffering on others.
Where are your scars

Where are your scars now,
Where are your scars now, wonderboys?

2020

The Fly

Surrounded as he is by the blood spatter
from the cut and thrust over an idea to which he was but briefly wed,
the fly is washing his hands of the matter

till the smoke clears. A wildcatter
on a rig still lumbering across the North Sea's bed,
surrounded as he is by the blood spatter

and spout of crude, he remembers only a scatter
of crudités, heavy hors d'oeuvres, glasses, remembers seeing red.
The fly is washing his hands of the matter

now a meal in an upper room has once again served to shatter
his illusions. Overcome by the high hum of the dead,
surrounded as he is by the blood spatter

from the cruets of oil and vinegar, the fly is tempted to spray attar
of roses on the aforesaid
"fly washing his hands of the matter,"

if only because the internet chatter
points to a city about to cede to the forces of Ethelred,
surrounded as it is. By the blood spatter

you shall know them as you shall know a satyr
by its horse's ears and tail. Instead
of washing his hands of the matter,

the fly might embrace an earth that is irredeemably in tatters
(a banquet of slivers and shreds
surrounded, as it is, by the interplanetary blood spatter),

might heed the pitter-patter
of unborn fly-feet on the stair tread.
But the fly is washing his hands of the matter

even as he contemplates a platter
complete with its severed head, now the centerpiece of the spread.
Surrounded as he is by the blood spatter
the fly is washing his hands of the matter.

2021

Beowulf, 114–169

"Under a new moon, Grendel set out"

Under a new moon, Grendel set out
to see what horde haunted this hall.
He found the Ring-Danes drunk,
douse-downed, making beds of benches.
They were mead-medicated, untroubled
by pain, their sleep untainted by sorrow.
Grendel hurt, and so he hunted. This stranger
taught the Danes about time. He struck, seized
thirty dreaming men, and hied himself home,
bludgeoning his burden as he bounded, for the Danes
had slept sweetly in a world that had woken him,
benefited from bounty, even as they'd broken him.

When golden teeth tasted the sky,
Grendel's silent skill was seen. His kills—
grim crimson spilt on banquet-boards.
The war-horde wailed at the spoiling of their sleep,
at the depths they'd dived in darkness, while their enemy ate.
A mournful morning. Their leader sat at his plate, old overnight,
impotent at this ingress. The band tracked the invader, but not to his lair.
They had prayers to call out, and pains to bear.
Grendel did not stay himself from slaughter. The next night
a second slaying, and then another, his rope played out and
rotted through, a cursed course plotted without mercy,
and corse after corse cold in his keep. Bro, it was easy
after that to count the weepers: men fleeing to cotes
beneath the king's wings. You'd have to have been a fool to miss
the malice of the Hell-dweller, now hall-dwelling. Those who lived, left—
or locked themselves in ladies' lodgings, far from fault lines.
Those who stayed? Slain.

For twelve snow-seasons, Grendel reigned over evening.
Hrothgar suffered, Heorot buffeted, no hero to hold it.
Every outsider talked shit, telling of legends and losses.
Hrothgar's hall became a morgue, dark marks on floorboards.
No songs, no scops, no searing meat, no blazing fire.
And Grendel, incomplete, raided relentlessly.
Dude, this was what they call a blood feud, a war
that tore a hole through the hearts of the Danes.
Grendel was broken, and would not brook peace,
desist in dealing deaths, or die himself.
He had no use for stealth—he came near-nightly,
and never negotiated. The old counselors knew better
than to expect a settlement in silver from him.
Ringless, Grendel's fingers, kingless,
his country. Be it wizened vizier or beardless boy,
he hunted them across foggy moors, an owl
mist-diving for mice, grist-grinding their tails
in his teeth. A hellion's home is anywhere
good men fear to tread; who knows the dread this
marauder mapped?

Grendel, enemy to everyone, waged his war
without an army, lonesome as he lapped
the luxurious lengths of Heorot. He howl-haunted
the hall at night, the gold-gifter's throne throwing
shade at him, his soul burning with dark flame.
He couldn't touch the treasure, or tame
his yearning, for he'd been spurned by God.

2020

Translated by Maria Dahvana Headley

francine j. harris

Oregon Trail, Missouri

O trail up outta here, how long ago
      you started to wander, crawling milkweed
through dependence, in grope toward sprawl
dominion. Rather red in your rove from southern transition,

thick of land use, what soft you carved of forest to get through
once dirt and fur and blood of original American and
bloody-scrape knuckles of emigrant pioneer. O what you woke
from sleep. dogwood drift loud and settling toward
expanse, like how a pride's breath

can move blossom to shiver and roll over false aster, shape
border from its river source, return to river as fat pocketbook, mussel
of critical habit, long breather and muscular foot
under cypress and promise of tree. O path for packed wagon

who dragged black slave alongside conduit, some salt
of new breeze, who swore deciduous freedom, and relented
only upon lawsuit in new land you opened to. O route
to burrow, you, like pipeline, leak the grease
of wayward stream. Trade off

and pick off growth in the way. How used, you. When
blue-promised god, some Negroes took up pack and white man's pack,
and given distance of black body to statehood pith, only made holy
states away. O what became you was over, the leaving grip bragged

all the way to the sea, already plundered and exhausted
of Shoshone patience and homesteading what hellbender
you've become. What uprooted clearing. stray cattle worth
whole encampments in fool's dust and deed. O what haven from man

who believe in America, only all to himself? Imagine

a way of shape that doesn't strangle. an arbor
of its very own leaf. Now, imagine
tern and piping plover that keeps expansion
      along its shore. a settlement for spring's deliver, not pipeline.

Imagine redbud staying put in its breeze and keeping us safely
strong as trees and dark as the bark of our open souls. Imagine
the park of evergreen surrender,
to a calmer, blue sky our govern might protect.

Imagine bald eagle again, not because white-headed
      but imagine bird, simple body of eager sea, talons
stretched over gold proportion. In summers, thick shiner.
In winter, undisturbed darter along somewhat snow, unstressed

by factory and loud humming fuel. O prairie of blazing star, imagine
full caves of left alone, unraided buffalo
clover, unhelped. unfringed orchid, unwestern. Imagine
      ground hallow, free to forage

its riverine root and plant vigor along the Missouri.

2020

The Butterflies the Mountain and the Lake

It's Saturday   most often neighbor   we
Are walking with our daughter lately   even when / We walk together
everywhere we go we want to go home everywhere   / But oh
hey did you see that story

about the butterflies the mountain and the lake
the   / Butterflies monarch butterflies huge swarms they
Migrate and as they migrate south   as they
Cross Lake Superior instead of flying

South straight across they fly
South over the water then fly east
still over the water then fly south   again / And now
biologists believe they   turn to avoid a mountain

That disappeared millennia ago   / No
butterfly lives long enough to fly   the whole migration
From the beginning to the end
they / Lay eggs along the way

Just as you and I   most often neighbor
Migrate together in our daughter   over a dark lake
We make with joy the child we make
And mountains are reborn in her

2022

They tear down my family home

As if sledgehammers weren't enough
the demolition men use their hands
to tear down the window djinn used to flit through
and with a kick the back door—even its memory—is gone.
Underfoot I feel the remains of the sugar loaves and oranges and mangoes
our furtive visitors hid under their black shawls.
They would come after evening prayer, the hems of their long jalabiyas
brushing across the threshold of the back door,
a door of gifts and sorceresses, now a door to nowhere.
The roof that never protected my childhood from the Delta rains
has reverted to its old self—a few trees you can count on one hand.

Now they're tearing down her old bedroom, casting into the air
strands of her still-wet hair, hair that slips through the cracks
of earthen walls about to become clods of dirt
as if no one had ever rested their back there.
Did my mother bathe before bed or at dawn?
Did she pull her hair from the comb's teeth to ward off
the evil eye, or fire, or the stratagems of neighbors?
My mother's hair slips away like a gift, or retribution.
What ties me to her now?
I donated her dresses to charity because they didn't fit me.
If we met, I'd be her older sister.
What ties me to her now? Her womb is with her in the ground—there
under the camphor tree, where early death is close enough to touch with
    your hand.

2022

Translated by Robyn Creswell

VALZHYNA MORT

Singer

A yolk of honey in a glass of cooling milk.
Bats playful like butterflies on power lines.
In all your stories blood hangs like braids

of drying onions. Our village is so small
it doesn't have its own graveyard. Our souls
are sapped in sour water of the bogs.

Men die in wars, their bodies their graves.
And women burn in fire. When midsummer
brings thunderstorms, we cannot sleep

because our house is a wooden sieve,
and crescent lightning cut off our hair.
The bogs ablaze, we sit all night in fear.

I always thought that your old trophy Singer,
would hurry us away on its arched back.
I thought we'd hold on to its mane of threads

from loosened spools along its Arabian spine,
the same threads that were sown into my skirts,
my underthings, first bras. What smell

came from those threads you had so long
sewn in, pulled out, sewn back into the clothes
that held together men who'd fall apart

undressed. The same threads between my legs!
I lash them, and the Singer gallops!

And sky hangs from the lightning's thread.
As in that poem: on Berlin's Jaegerstrasse
Aryan whores are wearing shirts ripped off
the sliced chests of our girls. My Singer-Horsey,

does everything have to be like a poem?

2020

Afternoons and Early Evenings

The beautiful golden days when you were soon to be dying
but could still enter into random conversations with strangers,
random but also deliberate, so impressions of the world
were still forming and changing you,
and the city was at its most radiant, uncrowded in summer
though by then everything was happening more slowly—
boutiques, restaurants, a little wine shop with a striped awning,
once a cat was sleeping in the doorway;
it was cool there, in the shadows, and I thought
I would like to sleep like that again, to have in my mind
not one thought. And later we would eat polpo and saganaki,
the waiter cutting leaves of oregano into a saucer of oil—
What was it, six o'clock? So when we left it was still light
and everything could be seen for what it was,
and then you got in the car—
Where did you go next, after those days,
where although you could not speak you were not lost?

2021

Meditation

Be good, O my Sorrow, try to be more calm.
You asked for Evening; Evening's here; it falls:
A darkling atmosphere enfolds the city,
Carrying peace to some, to others pain.

As the vile multitude of mortals go,
Under the whip of Pleasure, ruthless scourge,
In servile revels seeking out remorse,
My Sorrow, give me your hand; come this way,

Far from all that. See the dead years leaning
On heaven's balconies in dated dresses;
And rising from the waters, smiling Regret;

The dying sun sink sleepward under an arch.
And like a death shroud trailing in the East,
Hear, my dear, the gentle Night approaching.

2025

Translated by Nathaniel Rudavsky-Brody

Never Heaven

1.

Remember? Our faces still flushed
from the regions each in each had opened,
we stepped outside to find the time
had turned to snow:

soft approximate rooftops,
the parked car like a grounded cloud,
each particular tree limb, phone wire, fence post
more visible for having vanished.

2.

Do you remember
the hours' cashmere,

every pore aware,
novitiates of never?

It left us useless
for less.

2020

The Body Remembers

I stood on one foot for three minutes & didn't tilt
the scales. Do you remember how quickly

we scrambled up an oak leaning out over the creek,
how easy to trust the water to break

our glorious leaps? The body remembers
every wish one lives for or doesn't, or even horror.

Our dance was a rally in sunny leaves, then quick
as anything, Johnny Dickson was up opening

his wide arms in the tallest oak, waving
to the sky, & in the flick of an eye

he was a buffalo fish gigged, pleading
for help, voiceless. Bigger & stronger,

he knew every turn in the creek past his back door,
but now he was cooing like a brown dove

in a trap of twigs. A water-honed spear
of kindling jutted up, as if it were the point

of our folly & humbug on a Sunday afternoon, right?
Five of us carried him home through the thicket,

our feet cutting a new path, running in sleep
years later. We were young as condom-balloons

flowering crab apple trees in double bloom
& had a world of baleful hope & breath.

Does Johnny run fingers over the thick welt
on his belly, days we were still invincible?

Sometimes I spend half a day feeling for bones,
humming a half-forgotten ballad

on a park bench a long ways from home.
The body remembers the berry bushes

heavy with sweetness shivering in a lonely woods,
but I doubt it knows words live longer

than clay & spit of flesh, as rock-bottom love.
Is it easier to remember pleasure

or does hurt ease truest hunger?
Our summer, rocking back & forth, uprooting

what's to come, the shadow of the tree
weighed as much as a man.

2021

"Oceans could separate us, but no"

Oceans could separate us, but no
matter where we stand in them, we're
touching.

Can the same be said of the night sky?

*

I've always sought the pole furthest
from the one I know

*

In Australia, I was lost under the
Southern Cross.

*

But the reality is that I've never lived
more than a few hours from home.

2021

NELLY SACHS

"Dancer"

Dancer
like a bride
from blind space
you receive
the budding desire
of creation's distant days—

With your body's musical avenues
you graze on the air
there
where the earth
seeks new entry
to birth.

Through
night-lava
like eyelids
softly opening
the first cry
of creation's volcano
flickers.

In the branches of your limbs
the premonitions build
their twittering nests.

Like a milkmaid
in twilight
your fingertips tug
the secret sources

of light
till you—pierced by the
trial of evening—
deliver your eyes
to the moon, for the night-watch.

Dancer
twisting in labor
then spent
you alone
bear on your body's hidden cord
the God-given twinned jewels
of death and birth.

2022

Translated by Joshua Weiner

Pomegranates

Hard pomegranates half-ajar
Yielding to your brimming seeds,
I see the brows of lofty minds
Bursting with their discoveries!

If the fierce suns you ripened through,
O pomegranates half-agape,
Urged you, swelling up with pride,
To break your ruby-studded screens,

And your rind's desiccated gold
Rips open from an urgent force
Dissolving into scarlet jewels,

That luminescent rupture leads
A soul I had before to dream
Its hidden architecture's plan.

2020

Translated by Nathaniel Rudavsky-Brody

ADAM ZAGAJEWSKI

The Calling of St. Matthew

that priest looks just like Belmondo
—WISŁAWA SZYMBORSKA, *FUNERAL (II)*

—Look at his hand, his palm. Like a pianist's

—But that old guy can't see a thing

—What next, paying in a church

—Mom, my head aches

—Sharply individuated human figures

—Keep it down please, we can't focus

—The coins on the table, how much are they worth

—His operation's just three weeks away

—I'd say silver, definitely silver, but not pure

—Lord, how lovely

—To adorn the Contarelli Chapel

—Which one is Matthew, the young guy or the old?

—We almost got robbed on the subway today

—Two generations of European artists took it as their model

—Look, there's a cross in the window

—The light went out again

—The wall on the left is so black, like the world's end

—Have you got another euro or fifty cents?

—Can't be the young guy

—They're closing soon, hurry up

—He saw a man collecting taxes

—How much are these paintings insured for

—Jesus is in shadow but his face is light

—I'm leaving now, I'll wait outside

—Why don't they have a guard?

—They live in semi-darkness and suddenly there's light
—It's going out

Three Caravaggio masterpieces hang in a side chapel of the Church of San Luigi dei Francesi in Rome; you put coins in a meter to turn on the lights.

2022

Translated by Clare Cavanagh

DELMORE SCHWARTZ

Song

Fog in stony December: is it well,
The season's character being clear,
That every shape of error veil
Building and transient street-car. War
Fitly is made in summer, since it takes
The class of 1913 when they are
Immortal June. But still the buyer buys
His stocks, his sticks, his fur-coat, and such cakes
Still when the wind pursues its idiot fate,
Bearing the knife-edged cold and the radio's lies.

Beaded or smoky, much comfort is in fog,
Russia and Germany are near and far,
Dim in the subway, thunder and horror wait,
And all turn in their sleep to question where they are.

2023

This poem is previously unpublished.

---

in broad dayliGht black moms look grieving

a poem in response to Facebook comments

they have made hell
a home, on earth.

camera captures breath.
concrete captures body.
this is NOTHING
new.
yanking the limbs of breathless,
bleeding bodies behind backs.

i, too, yell commands to the deceased
the hole(y),
they seldom respond accordingly.
that is not a crime—
the yelling or the dying.
the shooting—that is the sin.

my mother says,
if you have a gun
you'll shoot a gun.
so, i don't have a gun
i think . . .
if you have a pen
you will shoot a pen.
i never thought a bullet
could write this many poems.

they do not sweat

when *they* grab *their* gun.

i do not sweat

when i grab my pen.

        the difference is in our bullets

                                  2020

A. E. STALLINGS

Apollo Takes Charge of His Muses

They sat there, nine women, much the same age,
The same poppy-red hair, and similar complexions
Freckling much the same in the summer glare,
The same bright eyes of green melting to blue
Melting to golden brown, they sat there,
Nine women, all of them very quiet, one,
Perhaps, was looking at her nails, one plaited
Her hair in narrow strands, one stared at a stone,
One let fall a mangled flower from her hands,
All nine of them very quiet, and the one who spoke
Said, softly:

"Of course he was very charming, and he smiled,
Introduced himself and said he'd heard good things,
Shook hands all round, greeted us by name,
Assured us it would all be much the same,
Explained his policies, his few minor suggestions
Which we would please observe. He looked forward
To working with us. Wouldn't it be fun? Happy
To answer any questions. Any questions? But
None of us spoke or raised her hand, and questions
There were none; what has poetry to do with reason
Or the sun?"

2023

What Was Poetry?

> I hate Christmas, but I hate people who hate
> Christmas even more.
> —JAMES SCHUYLER

No one really knew, though everyone knew what it *should* be;
And now it's just a way of being famous on a small scale.
It was supposed to be significant for its own sake,
Though that was never entirely true: human feelings
Got in the way, for while it was possible to remain unmoved
In the face of all that language, no one really wanted to:
They wanted to talk about it, to explain what it had let them see,
As though the world were incomplete before poetry filled it in.
And now there's nothing left to see: oh, poems come and go
And everyone complains about them, but, where there used to be
Arguments there's just appreciation and indifference,
Measured praise that's followed by forgetting. I'm as bad
As anyone: instead of reading I reread, instead of seeing
I remember, and instead of letting silence have its say
I fill it up with talk, as if the last word might be anything else.

And yet despite all this it matters. Sometimes in the midst
Of this long preparation for death that initial solitude returns
And the world seems actual and alive, as it assumes its opposite.
I think the truest thoughts are always second thoughts,
But who am I kidding, other than myself? I hope there's
Someone, that it casts its spell beyond the small cone of light
Hovering over my desk, and that what started out one night
So long ago in silence doesn't end that way. I fantasize
I can hear it somewhere in the realm of possibility,
But only now and then, in intervals between breaths.

2022

Postscript

And some time make the time to drive out west
Into County Clare, along the Flaggy Shore,
In September or October, when the wind
And the light are working off each other
So that the ocean on one side is wild
With foam and glitter, and inland among stones
The surface of a slate-grey lake is lit
By the earthed lightning of a flock of swans,
Their feathers roughed and ruffling, white on white,
Their fully grown headstrong-looking heads
Tucked or cresting or busy underwater.
Useless to think you'll park and capture it
More thoroughly. You are neither here nor there,
A hurry through which known and strange things pass
As big soft buffetings come at the car sideways
And catch the heart off guard and blow it open.

1996

Notes on the Poets

YEHUDA AMICHAI was born Ludwig Pfeuffer in Würzburg, Germany, on May 3, 1924. He moved with his family to Mandate Palestine in 1936, settling in Jerusalem. After serving in the 1948 Arab-Israeli War, he studied at Hebrew University and published his first book of poems, *Now and in Other Days*, in 1955. His first novel, *Not of This Time, Not of This Place*, was published in 1963, appearing in English in 1968. Ted Hughes, a longtime friend and collaborator, cotranslated the *Selected Poems* (1971) with Assia Gutmann and Harold Schimmel, which helped popularize his verse in the English-speaking world. Amichai's other translators into English include Robert Alter, Chana Bloch, Barbara Harshav, Benjamin Harshav, Chana Kronfeld, Stephen Mitchell, Daniel Weissbort, and Leon Wieseltier. He died in Jerusalem on September 22, 2000.

FSG published *The Poetry of Yehuda Amichai*, edited by Robert Alter, in 2015.

JOHN ASHBERY was born in Rochester, New York, on July 28, 1927. He attended Deerfield Academy and graduated from Harvard College in 1949. His first chapbook, *Turandot and Other Poems*, was published in 1953. *Some Trees* was awarded the Yale Younger Poets prize by W. H. Auden in 1956. He moved that year to France after receiving a Fulbright Fellowship, where he lived and worked as an art critic until returning to New York in 1965. In 1975, his book *Self-Portrait in a Convex Mirror* was awarded the Pulitzer Prize, the National Book Award, and the National Book Critics Circle Award. Ashbery would go on to win many other national and international awards in the course of his career. He died in Hudson, New York, on September 3, 2017.

Collections of Ashbery's work published by FSG include *And the Stars Were Shining* (1994), *Can You Hear, Bird* (1995), *Wakefulness* (1998), *Girls on the Run* (1999), *Your Name Here* (2000), and *Chinese Whispers* (2002), as well as reissues of *Houseboat Days* (1999, first published 1977), *A Wave* (1998, first published 1984), and *Hotel Lautréamont* (2000, first published 1992). In 2014, FSG published Ashbery's *Collected French Translations* of poetry and prose in two volumes, both edited by Rosanne Wasserman and Eugene Richie.

In 2017, FSG published *The Songs We Know Best*, a study of Ashbery's early life by Karin Roffman. She is currently at work on a full biography.

INGEBORG BACHMANN was born in Klagenfurt, Austria, on June 25, 1926. She received her PhD from the University of Vienna in 1949 and published her first collection of poems, *Die gestundete Zeit* (The day of reckoning), in 1953, for which she was awarded the Gruppe 47 Prize. She also wrote several libretti, radio plays, short stories, and a novel. She died in Rome on October 17, 1973.

FSG published a selection of her poems in English translation in *Twentieth-Century German Poetry: An Anthology* (2006), edited by Michael Hofmann.

CHARLES BAUDELAIRE was born in Paris on April 9, 1821. *Les Fleurs du mal*, his first volume of poems, appeared in 1857, and was followed by the posthumous *Le Spleen de Paris* in 1869. He died in Paris on August 31, 1867.

Nathaniel Rudavsky-Brody's translation of *Les Fleurs du mal* is forthcoming from FSG.

SYLVIE BAUMGARTEL was born in Edmonds, Washington, in 1976 and received an MFA from Bard College. She is the author of two books of poems, both published by FSG: *Song of Songs* (2019) and *Pink* (2021).

GOTTFRIED BENN was born near Putlitz, Germany, on May 2, 1886. His first chapbook, *Morgue und andere Gedichte* (Morgue and other poems), was published in 1912 while he was working as a pathologist in Berlin. At first sympathetic to National Socialism, his work was ultimately banned by the Nazis and subsequently by the Allies until the publication of *Statische Gedichte* (Static poems) in 1948. In his later years he was recognized as one of midcentury Germany's major poets and was nominated for the Nobel Prize on five occasions. He died in West Berlin on July 7, 1956.

In 2013, FSG published *Impromptus*, a selection of his poems translated and edited by Michael Hofmann.

CHARLES BERNSTEIN was born in New York City in 1950. He graduated from Harvard College in 1972 and published his first collection of poems, *Asylums*, in 1975. Between 1978 and 1981 he coedited the magazine *L=A=N=G=U=A=G=E*, which helped inaugurate the Language poetry movement.

All the Whiskey in Heaven, a selection of his poems, was published by FSG in 2010.

JOHN BERRYMAN was born John Allyn Smith, Jr., in McAlester, Oklahoma, on October 25, 1914. After his father's suicide in 1926, Berryman took his stepfather's name and lived with his mother in Massachusetts and New York City. He graduated from Columbia in 1936 before studying at Clare College, Cambridge, for two years. His first mature collection of verse, *The Dispossessed*, was published in 1948, and in 1956, Farrar, Straus and Cudahy published his book-length poem *Homage to Mistress Bradstreet*. Berryman's subsequent collections, all published by FSG, include *77 Dream Songs* (1964), which won the Pulitzer Prize, and *His Toy, His Dream, His Rest* (1968), which won the National Book Award and the Bollingen Prize. The 385 poems from these two books were compiled and published under the title *The Dream Songs* in 1969. Berryman died by suicide in Minneapolis, Minnesota, on January 7, 1972.

Berryman's other collections are *Love & Fame* (1970) and *Delusions, Etc.* (1972). His 1950 biography of Stephen Crane was reissued by Hill & Wang in 1982, and in 1989, FSG published his *Collected Poems*, edited by Charles Thornbury. In 1999, Berryman's writings on Shakespeare were published under the title *Berryman's Shakespeare* with an introduction by Robert Giroux. *The Heart Is Strange*, a new selection of his poems edited by Daniel Swift, was published to mark his centenary in 2014.

JOHN BETJEMAN was born in London on August 28, 1906. He studied at Magdalen College, Oxford, leaving without a degree. He published his first collection of poems while working as a radio broadcaster and as an editor at *The Architectural Review*, and came to wider attention for his *Collected Poems*, published in 1958. *Summoned by Bells*, an autobiography in blank verse, followed in 1960. Betjeman served as the Poet Laureate of the United Kingdom from 1972 until his death on May 19, 1984.

In 2006, FSG published an expanded edition of his *Collected Poems* and *Betjeman: A Life*, a biography by A. N. Wilson.

FRANK BIDART was born in Bakersfield, California, in 1939. He attended the University of California at Riverside and was a PhD candidate in English at Harvard, where he studied with and befriended Robert Lowell and became close to Elizabeth Bishop. His first collection of poems, *Golden State*, was published in 1973, followed by *The Book of the Body* (FSG, 1977) and *The Sacrifice* (Random House, 1983). In 1990, FSG published *In the Western Night*, a collection spanning the first twenty-five years of Bidart's career. FSG subsequently published *Desire* (1997), *Star Dust* (2005), *Watching the Spring Festival* (2008), and *Metaphysical Dog* (2013), which won the National Book Critics Circle Award. In 2017, FSG published *Half-light: Collected Poems, 1965–2016*, which was awarded the Pulitzer Prize for Poetry and the National Book Award. Bidart's most recent collection, *Against Silence*, was published in 2021. He lives in Cambridge, Massachusetts, and has taught at Wellesley College since 1972.

ELIZABETH BISHOP was born in Worcester, Massachusetts, on February 8, 1911. She attended the Walnut Hill School and entered Vassar College in 1929. After graduating in 1934, she traveled widely before moving to Key West in 1938, where she wrote many of the poems that would be published in her first collection, *North & South* (1946). An expanded edition of this book, *Poems: North & South—A Cold Spring*, appeared in 1955 while Bishop was living in Brazil, and was awarded the Pulitzer Prize for Poetry. In 1957, her translation of Alice Brant's *The Diary of Helena Morley* was published by Farrar, Straus and Cudahy. FSG published Bishop's *Questions of Travel* in 1965, followed by *The Complete Poems* (1969), which won the National Book Award, and *Geography III* (1976), which won the National Book Critics Circle

Award. She and Emanuel Brasil edited *An Anthology of Twentieth-Century Brazilian Poetry* in 1972. She died in Boston on October 6, 1979.

In 1983, FSG published a new edition of *The Complete Poems*, followed by the *Collected Prose* in 1984. *One Art*, a selection of Bishop's correspondence edited by Robert Giroux, was published in 1994. Other books published by FSG include *Exchanging Hats* (1996), a catalogue raisonné of Bishop's paintings, edited by William Benton; *Edgar Allan Poe & the Juke-Box* (2006), a collection of previously unpublished poems and drafts, edited by Alice Quinn; *Words in Air* (2008), Bishop's complete correspondence with Robert Lowell, edited by Thomas Travisano and Saskia Hamilton; and *Elizabeth Bishop and* The New Yorker (2011), her complete correspondence with her editors at the magazine, edited by Joelle Biele. Editions of Bishop's journals, her complete correspondence with Marianne Moore, and her correspondence with May Swenson are forthcoming from FSG.

LOUISE BOGAN was born in Livermore Falls, Maine, on August 11, 1897. She attended Girls' Latin School and entered Boston University in 1915, leaving after her first year. Her first collection of poems, *Body of This Death*, appeared in 1923. She served as poetry critic at *The New Yorker* from 1931 until near the end of her life. She died in New York City on February 4, 1970.

FSG published *The Blue Estuaries: Poems, 1923–1968*, in 1968.

YVES BONNEFOY, widely considered the leading poet of postwar France, was born in Tours on June 24, 1923. He studied at the University of Poitiers and the Sorbonne, and published his first of many collections of poems, *Du Mouvement et de l'immobilité de Douve* (*On the Motion and Immobility of Douve*), in 1953 (English translation 1968 by Galway Kinnell). In 1981, he assumed the chair previously held by Roland Barthes at the Collège de France. Bonnefoy died in Paris on July 1, 2016.

FSG published *The Curved Planks*, a bilingual edition of his poems with English translations by Hoyt Rogers, in 2006.

JOSEPH BRODSKY was born in Leningrad on May 24, 1940. He began writing and translating poetry at the age of fifteen, and in 1960 met Anna Akhmatova, who would become a friend and supporter. He was denounced for parasitism by a Leningrad newspaper in 1963 and sentenced to five years of hard labor the following year, though his sentence was commuted in 1965. He left the Soviet Union in 1972 with the help of W. H. Auden and settled in Ann Arbor, Michigan. He later taught at Mount Holyoke College in Massachusetts before moving to New York City. In 1987, he was awarded the Nobel Prize in Literature. Brodsky died in New York City on January 28, 1996.

Brodsky's first book to appear in English was *Elegy to John Donne and Other Poems* (1967). *A Part of Speech*, with translations by various hands, was published by FSG in 1980. Subsequent collections published by FSG include *To Urania* (1988) and *So Forth* (1996), which included both self-translated verse and original poems in English. The year 1996 also saw the publication of *Homage to Robert Frost*, a collaboration among Brodsky and his friends Seamus Heaney and Derek Walcott. Other works published by FSG include *Less Than One: Selected Essays* (1986), which won the National Book Critics Circle Award; the play *Marbles* (1989), translated by the author and Alan Myers; and the essay collections *Watermark* (1992) and *On Grief and Reason* (1995). In 2000, FSG published Brodsky's *Collected Poems in English*, followed by *Nativity Poems* (2001), featuring translations by Heaney, Walcott, Paul Muldoon, Anthony Hecht, and Richard Wilbur. *Selected Poems: 1968–1996*, edited by Ann Kjellberg, marked Brodsky's eightieth birthday in 2020.

ROSELLEN BROWN was born in Philadelphia in 1939 and studied at Barnard College and Brandeis University. *Some Deaths in the Delta*, her first book of poems, appeared in 1970, and was followed by *Cora Fry* in 1977. In 1994, FSG published *Cora Fry's Pillow Book*, a continuation of Brown's second book of poems. She is also the author of several novels and collections of stories, including *Before and After* (1992) and *Half a Heart* (2000).

PATRIZIA CAVALLI was born in Todi, Umbria, in 1949 and lives in Rome. Her first collection, *Le mie poesie non cambieranno il mondo* (*My Poems Won't Change the World*), was published in 1974 and followed by *Il cielo* (The sky) (1981) and *L'io singolare proprio mio* (The all mine singular I) (1992).

In 2013, FSG published a selected poems titled *My Poems Won't Change the World*, edited by Gini Alhadeff and featuring translations by Jorie Graham, Mark Strand, and others.

PAUL CELAN was born Paul Antschel in Cernowitz, then part of the Kingdom of Romania, on November 23, 1920. He left for France to study medicine in 1938, but returned to Romania before the start of World War II. His parents were deported to a Nazi concentration camp in 1942, where they both died. Celan was imprisoned in a forced labor camp until 1944. After the war, he lived in Bucharest and Vienna before settling in Paris, where he taught at the École normale supérieure and worked as a translator. His first collection of poems, *Der Sand aus den Urnen* (Sand from the urns), appeared in 1948, and was followed by *Mohn und Gedächtnis* (Poppy and memory) in 1952. Six more collections were published in German in his lifetime, along with two posthumous collections. He died in Paris on April 20, 1970.

Celan's first book to appear in English was *Speech-Grille and Selected Poems* (1971), translated by Joachim Neugroschel. Michael Hamburger translated several of his subsequent collections in English, among them his second, *Nineteen Poems* (1972). In 1986, *Last Poems*, translated by Katharine Washburn and Margaret Guillemin, was published by North Point Press.

Breathturn into Timestead: The Collected Later Poetry, featuring translations by

Pierre Joris, was published by FSG in 2014, followed by *Memory Rose into Threshold Speech: The Collected Earlier Poetry*, in 2020.

ELEANOR CHAI was born in New York City in 1967 and studied at Sarah Lawrence College and Harvard. She is the coeditor of the forthcoming *Efforts of Affection: The Correspondence of Elizabeth Bishop and Marianne Moore*.

FSG published her collection of poems, *Standing Water*, in 2016

JOHN CLARE was born in Helpston, Northamptonshire, on July 13, 1793. *Poems Descriptive of Rural Life and Scenery*, his first book, was published by John Taylor in London in 1820, followed by *The Village Minstrel* in 1821. He spent the final decades of his life in the Northampton General Lunatic Asylum, where he composed the poem "I Am" (published in 1848). Clare died on May 20, 1864.

In 2003, FSG published *"I Am": The Selected Poetry of John Clare*, edited by Jonathan Bate, to accompany his biography of the poet.

JEFF CLARK was born in Southern California in 1971. He received an MFA from the Iowa Writers' Workshop and published his first collection of poems, *The Little Door Slides Back*, in 1997.

FSG published his second collection, *Music and Suicide*, alongside a reissue of his first in 2004. In addition to Clark's poems, FSG has published many poetry titles featuring his cover designs.

KILLARNEY CLARY was born in Los Angeles in 1954 and received an MFA from the University of California, Irvine. FSG published her debut collection, *Who Whispered Near Me*, in 1989. She has written three subsequent books of poetry and lives in California.

LEONARD COHEN was born in Westmount, Quebec, a suburb of Montreal, on September 21, 1934. He entered McGill University in 1951 and published his first poems in 1954. His debut collection, *Let Us Compare Mythologies*, appeared in 1956, and was followed by the novels *The Favourite Game* (1963) and *Beautiful Losers* (1966). His first *Selected Poems* was published in 1968, by which time he had established himself as a musician. He wrote four more books of poems over the course of his later life and died in Los Angeles on November 17, 2016.

In 2018, FSG published *The Flame*, a selection of Cohen's poems, sketches, lyrics, and notebook excerpts edited by Robert Faggen and Alexandra Pleshoyano.

HENRI COLE was born in Fukuoka, Japan, in 1956. He was raised in Virginia and attended the College of William and Mary. His first collection of poems, *The Marble Queen*, appeared in 1986, and was followed by *The Zoo Wheel of Knowledge* (1989) and *The Look of Things* (1995). Cole teaches at Claremont McKenna College in California and lives in Boston.

In 1998, FSG published Cole's fourth collection, *The Visible Man.* His subsequent collections, all published by FSG, include *Middle Earth* (2003), *Blackbird and Wolf* (2007), *Pierce the Skin: Selected Poems, 1982–2007* (2010), *Touch* (2011), *Nothing to Declare* (2015), and *Blizzard* (2020).

PETER COLE was born in Paterson, New Jersey, in 1957. He attended Williams College and Hampshire College before moving to Israel in 1981. His books include *Rift* (1986), *Things on Which I've Stumbled* (2008), and *The Invention of Influence* (2014), as well as several collections of translations from Hebrew and Arabic. He teaches at Yale University and lives in Jerusalem and New Haven.

In 2017, FSG published *Hymns & Qualms: New and Selected Poems and Translations.*

AVERILL CURDY was born in Seattle in 1961 and received an MFA from the University of Houston and a PhD from the University of Missouri. FSG published her debut collection, *Song & Error*, in 2013. She teaches at Northwestern University and lives in Chicago.

MAHMOUD DARWISH, widely acknowledged as the national poet of Palestine, was born in the Galilean village of Birweh in 1941. His early poetry, published in the 1960s, earned him the sobriquet "Poet of the Resistance." After several stints in prison and a period of house arrest, he left Palestine to study in the Soviet Union in 1970 and lived the remainder of his life in exile in Cairo, Beirut, and Paris. His memoir of life in Beirut during the Israeli siege of 1982, *Memory for Forgetfulness* (1986), is among the prose masterworks of modern Arabic. He died in Houston, Texas, on August 9, 2008.

FSG published *If I Were Another*, a selection of his late poems translated by Fady Joudah, in 2009.

LYDIA DAVIS was born in Northampton, Massachusetts, in 1947 and studied at Barnard College. Her first book of stories, *The Thirteenth Woman, and Other Stories*, appeared in 1976. She is also a noted translator from the French, and has published translations of Maurice Blanchot, Proust, and Flaubert.

Among her books published by FSG are *Break It Down* (1986), *The End of the Story* (1995), *Almost No Memory* (1997), *Varieties of Disturbance* (2007), and *Can't and Won't* (2014). In 2009, FSG published *The Collected Stories of Lydia Davis*, followed by *Essays One* (2019) and *Essays Two* (2021). She was awarded the Man Booker International Prize in 2013.

CARLOS DRUMMOND DE ANDRADE was born in Itabira, Brazil, on October 31, 1902. He studied pharmacy in Belo Horizonte and worked as a civil servant for much of his life. His first collection of poems appeared in 1930, and his first collection in English, *Souvenir of the Ancient World*, was translated by Mark Strand and published in 1976. Drummond died in Rio de Janeiro on August 17, 1987.

In 2015, FSG published *Multitudinous Heart*, a selection of his poems translated by Richard Zenith.

CAROL ANN DUFFY was born in Glasgow in 1955. She entered the University of Liverpool in 1974 and published her first mature book of verse, *Standing Female Nude*, in 1985. Her other significant early collections are *Selling Manhattan* (1987), *The Other Country* (1990), and *Mean Time* (1993). Faber and Faber, Inc., published *The World's Wife* in the United States in 2000 (first FSG paperback edition, 2001), followed by *Feminine Gospels* in 2003 (FSG paperback, 2005). Duffy served as Poet Laureate of the United Kingdom from 2009 to 2019.

In 2013, FSG published *Rapture* (originally published in 2005) and a new collection, *The Bees*.

STUART DYBEK was born in Chicago in 1942. He received an MFA from the Iowa Writers' Workshop and published his first collection of poems, *Brass Knuckles*, in 1979. In 2004, FSG published his second collection of poems, *Streets in Their Own Ink*. Dybek is also the author of a novel and two collections of stories published by FSG: *I Sailed With Magellan* (2003), *Paper Lantern: Love Stories* (2014), and *Ecstatic Cahoots: Fifty Short Stories* (2014).

T. S. ELIOT was born in Saint Louis, Missouri, on September 26, 1888. He graduated from Harvard College in 1909 and continued his studies at the Sorbonne, Harvard, and Merton College, Oxford, before settling permanently in England, where he worked as a teacher and banker before founding the literary review *The Criterion* and becoming a director at Faber and Gwyer, later Faber and Faber. His poem "The Love Song of J. Alfred Prufrock" appeared in *Poetry* in 1915 at the urging of Ezra Pound. "The Wasteland" was published in *The Criterion* in 1922, and in 1925 Eliot collected the poems in his first chapbook, *Prufrock and Other Observations* (1917), along with "The Wasteland" and "The Hollow Men," in a volume titled *Poems: 1909–1925*, published by Faber and Faber. Eliot's other major works include "Ash Wednesday" (1930) and the *Four Quartets* (1936–1942); *Old Possum's Book of Practical Cats* (1939); *The Sacred Wood* (1920), a collection of literary criticism; and the plays *Sweeney Agonistes* (1932), *Murder in the Cathedral* (1935), and *The Family Reunion* (1939). He was awarded the Nobel Prize in Literature in 1948 and died in London on January 4, 1965.

Eliot was first published by Farrar, Straus and Cudahy in 1956, when his poem "The Cultivation of Christmas Trees" appeared in a stand-alone illustrated edition.

This was followed by *On Poetry and Poets* (1957) and the play *The Elder Statesman* (1959). In 1964, FSG released the first published edition of Eliot's doctoral thesis, *Knowledge and Experience in the Philosophy of F. H. Bradley*. *To Criticize the Critic and Other Writings* and *Poems Written in Early Youth* appeared in 1965 and 1967, respectively.

In 2018, FSG published *The Poems of T. S. Eliot* in two volumes, edited by Christopher Ricks and Jim McCue.

LUCIANO ERBA was born in Milan on September 18, 1922, where he studied at the Università Cattolica del Sacro Cuore. His debut collection, *Linea K*, appeared in 1951. *The Greener Meadow: Selected Poems*, translated by Peter Robinson, was published by Princeton University Press in 2006. Erba also translated a number of works by poets writing in English and French, including Thom Gunn and Blaise Cendrars. He died in Milan on August 3, 2010.

Erba's work appeared in *The FSG Book of Twentieth-Century Italian Poetry* (2012).

MARIE ÉTIENNE was born in France in 1938. In 2008, FSG published *King of a Hundred Horsemen*, translated by Marilyn Hacker. She lives in Paris.

JAMES FENTON was born in Lincoln, England, in 1949. He studied at Magdalen College, Oxford, and later served as Oxford's Professor of Poetry from 1994 to 1999. His Newdigate Prize–winning poem *Our Western Furniture* appeared as a pamphlet in 1968, and his first full-length book, *Terminal Moraine*, was published in 1972. Fenton spent much of the 1970s in Southeast Asia writing about the conflicts in Vietnam and Cambodia. He has also written theater, art, and literary criticism; plays; and libretti.

Fenton's *Children in Exile: Poems, 1968–1984* was published by FSG in 1994, alongside a new collection, *Out of Danger*. His *Selected Poems* was published in 2006. FSG has also published a number of works of nonfiction by Fenton, including *Leonardo's Nephew* (1998), *The Strength of Poetry* (2001), *A Garden from a Hundred Packets of Seed* (2002), *An Introduction to English Poetry* (2003), and *The Love Bomb* (2003). A collected edition of his poems and a study of interior decoration are forthcoming. He lives in New York City.

DAVID FERRY was born in 1924 in Orange, New Jersey. He studied at Amherst and Harvard and taught for many years at Wellesley College. Ferry published his first collection of poems, *On the Way to the Island*, in 1960. *Bewilderment: New Poems and Translations* (2012) received the National Book Award. His version of Virgil's *Aeneid* was published by the University of Chicago Press in 2017.

FSG has published Ferry's translations of *Gilgamesh* (1992), Horace's *Odes* (1997) and *Epistles* (2001), and Virgil's *Eclogues* (1999) and *Georgics* (2005).

ROBERT FITZGERALD was born in Geneva, New York, on October 12, 1910. He attended the Choate School and Harvard College, graduating in 1933. His first collection of original poems was published in 1935, and his first translation, Euripides's *Alcestis* (with Dudley Fitts), appeared the following year. His translation of Homer's *The Odyssey* was first published in 1961, and was republished by FSG in 1998; his 1974 translation of *The Iliad* was republished by FSG in 2004. His version of Virgil's *Aeneid* was published by Random House in 1983. Fitzgerald served as Boylston Professor of Rhetoric at Harvard from 1965 to 1981. He died in Hamden, Connecticut, on January 16, 1985.

MICHAEL FRIED was born in New York City in 1939 and studied at Princeton, Harvard, and Merton College, Oxford. He was professor of art history at Johns Hopkins and has written numerous books of history and criticism. Fried published his first collection of poems, *Powers*, in 1973.

FSG published his second collection of verse, *To the Center of the Earth*, in 1994.

FEDERICO GARCÍA LORCA was born in Fuente Vaqueros, Granada, Spain, on June 5, 1898. He entered the University of Granada in 1915 and moved to Madrid in 1919, where he compiled his first *Libro de poemas* (Book of poems) (1921). His best-known collection, *Romancero gitano* (*Gypsy Ballads*), appeared in 1928, before Lorca's departure for the United States the following year. *Poeta en Nueva York* (*Poet in New York*), inspired by his time in the city, was published posthumously in 1940. Lorca returned to Spain in 1930, and wrote his most celebrated plays while touring the country under the aegis of the Second Spanish Republic. He was assassinated by Francoist troops outside Granada on August 19, 1936.

In 1988, FSG published a new edition of *Poet in New York*, edited by Christopher Maurer and translated by Greg Simon and Steven F. White. FSG's edition of Lorca's *Collected Poems*, also edited by Maurer, appeared in 1991, followed by *Three Plays* (1993), *Selected Verse* (1996), and the play *Blood Wedding* (1997), in a new version by Ted Hughes.

LOUISE GLÜCK was born in New York City in 1943 and studied poetry at Sarah Lawrence College and Columbia University. Her debut collection of poems, *Firstborn*, appeared in 1968, followed by *The House on Marshland* (1975) and *Descending Figure* (1980). Her subsequent collections include *The Triumph of Achilles* (1985), which won the National Book Critics Circle Award; *Ararat* (1990); *The Wild Iris* (1992), which won the Pulitzer Prize for Poetry; *Meadowlands* (1996); *Vita Nova* (1999); and *The Seven Ages* (2001).

Books published by FSG include *Averno* (2006), *A Village Life* (2009), *Poems 1962–2012* (2012, in conjunction with Ecco Press), *Faithful and Virtuous Night* (2014), which won the National Book Award for Poetry, and *American Originality* (2017), a collection of essays. In 2020, Glück was awarded the Nobel Prize in Literature. *Winter Recipes from the Collective* was published in 2021.

SIDNEY GOLDFARB was born in Peabody, Massachusetts, in 1942 and attended Harvard College. FSG published two collections of his poems: *Speech, for Instance* (1969) and *Messages* (1971).

ELIZA GRISWOLD was born in 1973. She attended Princeton University and published her first chapbook, *A Night Full of Low Stars*, in 1997. Her subsequent books, all published by FSG, include the poetry collections *Wideawake Field* (2007) and *If Men, Then* (2020); *I Am the Beggar of the World: Landays from Contemporary Afghanistan* (2014), which won the PEN Award for Poetry in Translation; and the nonfiction works *The Tenth Parallel* (2010) and *Amity and Prosperity* (2018), which was awarded the Pulitzer Prize.

DURS GRÜNBEIN was born in Dresden in 1962. He moved to Berlin in 1985 and published his first collection of poems in 1988. He has also translated the work of numerous poets including John Ashbery and Wallace Stevens.

FSG has published two of his books in English: *Ashes for Breakfast: Selected Poems* (2005), translated by Michael Hofmann, and *The Bars of Atlantis: Selected Essays* (2010), edited by Michael Eskin and translated by Hofmann, John Crutchfield, and Andrew Shields.

THOM GUNN was born in Gravesend, England, on August 29,1929. He studied at Trinity College, Cambridge, and published his first collection of verse, *Fighting Terms*, in 1954. That same year he moved to California, where he would spend the rest of his life. Gunn's subsequent collections include *The Sense of Movement* (1957) and *My Sad Captains* (1961), the latter of which FSG republished with *Moly* (1971) in 1973.

Other books published by FSG include *Jack Straw's Castle* (1976), Gunn's first *Selected Poems* (1979), *The Occasions of Poetry* (essays, 1982), *The Passages of Joy* (1982), *The Man with Night Sweats* (1992), *Collected Poems* (1994), and *Boss Cupid* (2000). Gunn died in San Francisco on April 25, 2004.

In 2009, FSG published a second *Selected Poems*, edited by August Kleinzahler, followed by the *New Selected Poems*, edited by Clive Wilmer, in 2018. A selection of his letters, edited by Michael Nott, who is also writing a biography of the poet, will appear in 2022.

francine j. harris was born in Detroit in 1972 and received an MFA from the University of Michigan. *allegiance*, her first collection of poems, appeared in 2012, and was followed by *play dead* (2016). She teaches at the University of Houston.

Here is the Sweet Hand, her third book of poems, was published by FSG in 2020 and received the National Book Critics Circle Award.

TONY HARRISON was born in Leeds, England, in 1937, where he attended university. His first full-length book of verse, *The Loiners*, was published in 1970. His major poetic works include "V" (1985), *The Gaze of the Gorgon* (1992), which was adapted for television, and *The Shadow of Hiroshima* (1995). He has also written numerous dramatic works, many of them adaptations of classical plays, including *The Trackers of Oxyrhynchus* (1988) and *The Labourers of Herakles* (1995).

FSG published *V. and Other Poems* in 1990.

MARIA DAHVANA HEADLEY was born in Estacada, Oregon, in 1977 and attended New York University. In 2018, MCD/FSG published *The Mere Wife*, an adaptation of *Beowulf*, followed by her verse translation of the same in 2020.

SEAMUS HEANEY was born on his family's farm near Castledawson, Northern Ireland, on April 13, 1939, and moved with his family to nearby Bellaghy in 1953. He entered Queen's University Belfast in 1957, working as a teacher after graduation. His first collection of poems, *Death of a Naturalist*, was published to widespread acclaim by Faber and Faber in 1966, and was first published in the United States in 1969. Heaney's collections published by Faber and Faber, Inc., in the United States are *Door into the Dark* (1972, first published 1969), *Wintering Out* (1972), and *North* (1975). FSG published *Field Work* (1979), *Station Island* (1985, first published 1984), *The Haw Lantern* (1987), *Seeing Things* (1991), *The Spirit Level* (1996), *Electric Light* (2001), *District and Circle* (2006), and *Human Chain* (2010). In 1985, Heaney was awarded the Nobel Prize in Literature. He died in Dublin on August 30, 2013.

In addition to his poems, FSG has published several collections of Heaney's prose: *Preoccupations* (1980), *The Government of the Tongue* (1989), *The Redress of Poetry* (1995), and *Finders Keepers: Selected Prose, 1971–2001* (2002), as well as a version of Sophocles's *Philoctetes, The Cure at Troy* (1991). FSG also published several translations by Heaney: *Sweeney Astray* (1984), *Sweeney's Flight* (1992), *Beowulf* (2000), and book VI of the *Aeneid* (2016). Selections of his poems published by FSG include *Poems, 1965–1975* (1980), *Selected Poems, 1966–1987* (1990; reissued 2014) *Opened Ground: Poems, 1966–1996* (1998), *Selected Poems, 1988–2013* (2014), and, most recently, *100 Poems* (2019). Collected editions of his letters, poems, and translations, as well as a biography by Fintan O'Toole, are forthcoming.

HERMANN HESSE was born in Calw, Kingdom of Württemberg, on July 2, 1877. He published his first book, a collection of poems titled *Romantische Lieder* (Romantic songs), in 1899; though known primarily as a novelist, Hesse would continue writing poems throughout his life. He received the Nobel Prize in Literature in 1946 and died in Montagnola, Switzerland, on August 9, 1962.

In 1970, FSG published *Poems*, a selection of his work edited and translated by James Wright.

DAVID HINTON was born in 1954. He studied Chinese at Cornell University and has translated the work of several major poets, including Tu Fu, Li Po, Meng Chiao,

Xie Lingyun, and Po Chü-i, as well as Bei Dao. He has also translated Zhuang Zhou, *The Analects* of Confucius, and Mencius. *Desert*, a collection of original poems, was published in 2018. He lives in Vermont.

FSG published his *Classical Chinese Poetry: An Anthology* in 2008, followed by his translation of the *I Ching* in 2015.

MICHAEL HOFMANN was born in 1957 in Freiburg, West Germany. He was raised in England and Scotland and studied at Winchester College and Cambridge University. His first collection of poems, *Nights in the Iron Hotel*, was published by Faber and Faber in 1983. *Approximately Nowhere* was published in the United States by Faber and Faber, Inc., in 1999.

Collections published by FSG include Hofmann's *Selected Poems* (2009) and *One Lark, One Horse* (2019), in addition to the essay collections *Behind the Lines* (2002) and *Where Have You Been?* (2014). Hofmann has also translated numerous authors from the German, including two poets published by FSG, Gottfried Benn and Durs Grünbein. He and James Lasdun coedited *After Ovid: New Metamorphoses* (FSG, 1995), a collection of contemporary versions of myths from the *Metamorphoses* by poets including Seamus Heaney, Thom Gunn, Ted Hughes, Paul Muldoon, and Frederick Seidel. He is also the editor of *Twentieth-Century German Poetry: An Anthology*, published by FSG in 2006.

RICHARD HOWARD was born in Cleveland in 1929. He studied at Columbia University and the Sorbonne and published his first collection of poems, *Quantities*, in 1962. He was awarded the Pulitzer Prize for this third collection of poems, *Untitled Subjects* (1969). He has also translated numerous works from the French, winning a National Book Award for his 1982 translation of Baudelaire's *Les Fleurs du mal*.

In 2004, FSG published *Inner Voices: Selected Poems, 1963–2003* and *Paper Trail: Selected Prose, 1965–2003*.

TED HUGHES was born in West Yorkshire on August 17, 1930. He studied at Pembroke College, Cambridge, and worked odd jobs there and in London after graduation. He married the poet Sylvia Plath in 1956 and published his first collection of poems, *The Hawk in the Rain*, with Faber and Faber in 1957. His other important early works include *Lupercal* (1960), *Crow* (1970), and *Moortown* (1979).

Collections published by FSG include *Wolfwatching* (1991, first published 1989), *Tales from Ovid* (1997), *Birthday Letters* (1998), *Selected Poems: 1957–1994* (2002), *Collected Poems* (2003, edited by Paul Keegan), and *A Ted Hughes Bestiary* (2016). FSG has also published Hughes's translations of Federico García Lorca's *Blood Wedding* (1997), Euripides's *Alcestis* (1999), and Aeschylus's *Oresteia* (2000); a further selection of his translations edited by Daniel Weissbort (2007); the *Letters of Ted Hughes*, edited by Christopher Reid (2008); the nonfiction works *Shakespeare and the*

Goddess of Complete Being (1992) and *A Dancer to God* (1993); and the anthology *A Choice of Shakespeare's Verse* (2007).

Hughes served as Poet Laureate of the United Kingdom from 1984 until his death in London on October 28, 1998.

ISHION HUTCHINSON was born in Port Antonio, Jamaica, in 1983. He received an MFA from New York University and now teaches at Cornell. He published his first collection of poems, *Far District*, in 2010. In 2016, FSG published his second collection, *House of Lords and Commons*, which received the National Book Critics Circle Award for poetry. A collection of his essays, *Fugitive Tilts*, and a new edition of *Far District* are forthcoming from FSG in 2022.

MAX JACOB was born in Quimper, Brittany, on July 12, 1876. He moved to Paris as a young man, where he became part of a circle that included Pablo Picasso and Guillaume Apollinaire. Among his most important works are the prose poem *The Dice Cup* and *Le laboratoire central* (The Central Laboratory), a collection of free verse. He left Paris for the Loire Valley in 1936, where he lived until being arrested by the Gestapo in 1944. He died at the Drancy concentration camp on March 5, 1944.

John Ashbery's translations of Jacob's work appeared in *Collected French Translations: Poetry* (FSG, 2014).

RANDALL JARRELL was born in Nashville on May 6, 1914, and graduated from Vanderbilt University in 1935. He subsequently taught at Kenyon College, where he befriended Robert Lowell, and published his first collection of poems, *Blood for a Stranger*, in 1942, the year he joined the air force. His collection *The Woman at the Washington Zoo* (1960) received the National Book Award for Poetry. He died in Chapel Hill, North Carolina, on October 14, 1965.

In 1967, FSG published *Randall Jarrell, 1914–1965*, a memorial volume edited by Lowell, Peter Taylor, and Robert Penn Warren. In 1969, FSG published *The Complete Poems* and *The Third Book of Criticism*, followed by Jarrell's translation of Goethe's *Faust* (1976); *Kipling, Auden & Co.: Essays and Reviews* (1980); and a *Selected Poems* (1990), edited by William H. Pritchard.

JUAN RAMÓN JIMÉNEZ was born in Moguer, Andalusia, Spain, on December 23, 1881. He studied law at the University of Seville before turning to poetry, publishing his first two books at the age of eighteen. He left Spain in 1936, eventually settling in Puerto Rico, and was awarded the Nobel Prize in Literature in 1956. Jiménez died in San Juan on May 29, 1958.

In 1957, FSG published his *Selected Writings* in English, translated by H. R. Hays.

DEVIN JOHNSTON was born in Canton, New York, in 1970 and raised in North Carolina. He studied at Oberlin College and the University of Chicago and teaches at

Saint Louis University. Johnston is the coeditor of Flood Editions. His first collection of poems, *Telepathy*, was published in 2001, and was followed by *Aversions* (2004) and *Sources* (2008). His subsequent collections, all published by FSG, include *Traveler* (2011), *Far-Fetched* (2015), and *Mosses and Lichens* (2019).

LAWRENCE JOSEPH was born in Detroit in 1948. He studied at the University of Michigan and Magdalene College, Cambridge, and published his first collection of poems, *Shouting at No One*, in 1983. Collections published by FSG include *Before Our Eyes* (1993), *Into It* and *Codes, Precepts, Biases, and Taboos: Poems, 1973–1993* (2005), *So Where Are We?* (2017), and *A Certain Clarity: Selected Poems* (2020), in addition to a work of nonfiction, *Lawyerland* (1997). He lives and teaches law at St. John's University in New York City.

AUGUST KLEINZAHLER was born in Jersey City in 1949 and raised in Fort Lee. He studied under Basil Bunting at the University of Victoria in British Columbia and published his first book of poems, *The Sausage Master of Minsk*, in 1977. His other early collections include *A Calendar of Airs* (1978), *Storm Over Hackensack* (1985), and *Earthquake Weather* (1989).

Collections published by FSG include *Red Sauce, Whiskey, and Snow* (1995), *Green Sees Things in Waves* (1998), *Live from the Hong Kong Nile Club: Poems, 1975–1990* (2000), *The Strange Hours Travelers Keep* (2003), the National Book Critics Circle Award–winning *Sleeping It Off in Rapid City* (2008), *The Hotel Oneira* (2013), *Before Dawn on Bluff Road / Hollyhocks in the Fog: Selected New Jersey Poems / Selected San Francisco Poems* (2017), and *Snow Approaching on the Hudson* (2020). Prose works published by FSG include *Cutty, One Rock* (2004) and *Sallies, Romps, Portraits, and Send-Offs: Selected Prose, 2000–2016* (2017). He lives in San Francisco.

BILL KNOTT was born in Carson City, Michigan, on February 17, 1960. His first collection, *The Naomi Poems: Corpse and Beans*, was published under the nom de plume Saint Geraud in 1968. Among his other books are *Becos* (1983) and *Outremer* (1989). Knott taught at Emerson College in Boston for more than twenty-five years and died in Bay City, Michigan, on March 12, 2014.

FSG published two of Knott's collections of poems: *The Unsubscriber* (2004) and *I Am Flying into Myself: Selected Poems, 1960–2014*, edited by Thomas Lux (2017).

JOHN KOETHE was born in San Diego in 1945 and received a BA from Princeton and a PhD from Harvard. His early books of poems include *Blue Vents* (1968) and *Domes* (1973). He is an emeritus professor of philosophy at the University of Wisconsin–Milwaukee.

Collections published by FSG include *The Swimmer* (2016) and *Walking Backwards: Poems, 1966–2016* (2018). A new collection, *Beyond Belief*, will be published in 2022.

YUSEF KOMUNYAKAA was born in Bogalusa, Louisiana, in 1947. He served in the Vietnam War as managing editor of the *Southern Cross*, a military paper, and later received his MFA from the University of California, Irvine. His first collection, *Dedications & Other Darkhorses*, appeared in 1977. Subsequent important collections include *Copacetic* (1984), *Dien Cai Dau* (1988), and *Neon Vernacular: New and Selected Poems* (1993), for which he was awarded the Pulitzer Prize.

Books published by FSG include *Talking Dirty to the Gods* (2000), *Taboo* (2004), *Warhorses* (2008), *The Chameleon Couch* (2011), *The Emperor of Water Clocks* (2015), and *Everyday Mojo Songs of Earth: New and Selected Poems, 2001–2021* (2021). He teaches at New York University.

ALEKSANDR KUSHNER was born in Leningrad in 1936. He studied at Herzen University and published his first book of poems in 1962, joining the Union of Soviet Writers in 1965.

In 1991, FSG published *Apollo in the Snow: Selected Poems, 1960–1987*, translated by Paul Graves and Carol Ueland, followed by a second selection, *Apollo in the Grass* (2015), translated by Ueland and Robert Carnevale.

PHILIP LARKIN was born in Coventry, England, on August 9, 1922. He studied at Saint John's College, Oxford, and published his first book of poems, *The North Ship*, in 1945. His first mature work, collected in *The Less Deceived*, appeared in 1955, followed by *The Whitsun Weddings* in 1964 and *High Windows*, which was published by FSG in 1974. FSG published two collections of Larkin's prose: *Required Writing* (1984) and *All What Jazz: A Record Diary* (1985). He died in Hull, England, on December 2, 1985. In 1989, FSG published Larkin's *Collected Poems*, followed by his *Selected Letters* (1993), both edited by Anthony Thwaite. *The Complete Poems*, edited by Archie Burnett, was published by FSG in 2012. Andrew Motion's biography of the poet was published by FSG in 1993.

JAMES LASDUN was born in London in 1958 and studied at Bristol University. His debut collection of poems, *A Jump Start*, was published in 1987, and in 2015, FSG published *Bluestone: New and Selected Poems*. Lasdun has also written numerous novels, short story collections, and works of nonfiction, several of which have been published by FSG: *Three Evenings* (1992), *It's Beginning to Hurt* (2009), *Give Me Everything You Have* (2013), and a new edition of his 2002 debut novel, *The Horned Man* (2013). He is the coeditor, with Michael Hofmann, of *After Ovid: New Metamorphoses* (FSG, 1995).

GIACOMO LEOPARDI, who is generally considered Italy's first modern poet, was born in Recanati, in the Papal States, on June 29, 1798, and died in Naples on June 14, 1837.

In 2010, FSG published a bilingual edition of Leopardi's *Canti*, translated and introduced by Jonathan Galassi. In 2015, FSG also brought out the first complete English edition of his great notebook, the *Zibaldone*, translated by Kathleen Baldwin, Richard Dixon, David Gibbons, Ann Goldstein, Gerard Slowey, Martin Thom, and Pamela Williams.

CHRISTOPHER LOGUE was born in Portsmouth, England, on November 23, 1926. Beginning in the late 1950s, he published a series of modernist adaptations of Homer's *Iliad*, the work for which he is best known. His *Selected Poems* was published by Faber and Faber in 1996. Logue died in London on December 2, 2011.

Beginning in 1990, FSG published several installments of his version of the *Iliad*: *War Music*, *Kings* (1991), *The Husbands* (1995), and *All Day Permanent Red* (2003). In 2016, FSG collected unpublished and previously published portions of this work in a single volume titled *War Music*, edited by Christopher Reid.

ROBERT LOWELL was born in Boston on March 1, 1917. He attended St. Mark's School and entered Harvard College in 1935, graduating from Kenyon College in 1940. His first full-length book, *Lord Weary's Castle*, won the Pulitzer Prize for Poetry in 1947. *Life Studies* was published by Farrar, Straus and Cudahy in 1959 and won the 1960 National Book Award. His subsequent collections, all published by FSG, were *Imitations* (1961); *For the Union Dead* (1964); *Near the Ocean* (1967); *Notebook 1967–68* (1969 and 1970); *History* (1973); *For Lizzie and Harriet* (1973); *The Dolphin* (1973), which received the Pulitzer Prize; *Selected Poems* (1976); and *Day by Day* (1977), which received the National Book Critics Circle Award. Lowell also published a number of plays and works in translation with FSG. He died in New York City on September 12, 1977.

FSG published Lowell's *Collected Prose*, edited by Robert Giroux, in 1987, and his *Collected Poems*, edited by Frank Bidart and David Gewanter, in 2003. His complete correspondence with Elizabeth Bishop, *Words in Air*, edited by Thomas Travisano and Saskia Hamilton, appeared in 2008. FSG issued a *New Selected Poems*, edited by Katie Peterson, in celebration of the poet's centenary in 2017. *The Dolphin Letters*, a collection of letters by Lowell, Elizabeth Hardwick, and others about the controversy surrounding *The Dolphin*, also edited by Saskia Hamilton, was published in 2019. An edition of his *Memoirs*, edited by Steven Gould Axelrod and Grzegorz Kość, will appear in 2022.

MINA LOY was born in London on December 27, 1882. She studied art in Munich and Paris, where she would eventually publish her first book of poems, *Lunar Baedeker*, in 1923. She died in Aspen, Colorado, on September 25, 1966.

In 1996, FSG published *The Lost Lunar Baedeker*, an authoritative edition of her work edited by Roger L. Conover, as well as *Becoming Modern*, a biography by Carolyn Burke.

VALERIO MAGRELLI was born in Rome in 1957. He studied at the University of Rome La Sapienza and published his first book of poems, *Ora serrata retinae*, in 1980. He has translated Mallarmé, Verlaine, and Valéry, and written several critical works on French poetry.

In 2010, FSG published *Vanishing Points*, a selection of his poems translated by Jamie McKendrick.

ROYA MARSH was born in the Bronx, New York, in 1988 and studied at Iona College. In 2020, FSG published her debut collection of poems, *dayliGht*.

GLYN MAXWELL was born in 1962 in Welwyn Garden City, England. He studied at Oxford and at Boston University under Derek Walcott and published his first book of poems, *Tale of the Mayor's Son*, in 1990.

In 2011, FSG published *One Thousand Nights and Counting: Selected Poems*. Maxwell also edited *The Poetry of Derek Walcott* (2014) and is in the course of translating Joseph Brodsky's early verse.

SHANE MCCRAE was born in Portland, Oregon, in 1975. He received an MFA from the Iowa Writers' Workshop in 2004 and a JD from Harvard Law School in 2007 and published his first full-length book of poems, *Mule*, in 2010. His 2017 collection, *In the Language of My Captor*, was a finalist for the National Book Award.

Collections published by FSG include *The Gilded Auction Block* (2019) and *Sometimes I Never Suffered* (2020). A new book, *Cain Named the Animal*, is forthcoming in 2022. He teaches at Columbia University and lives in New York City.

MAUREEN N. MCLANE was born in 1967 in upstate New York. She attended Harvard College and Oxford University and received her PhD from the University of Chicago. She is professor of English at New York University.

Her first full-length book of poems, *Same Life*, was published by FSG in 2008. Subsequent collections, all published by FSG, include *World Enough* (2010), *This Blue* (2014), *Mz N: the serial* (2016), *Some Say* (2017), and *More Anon: Selected Poems* (2021). She is also the author of the nonfiction work *My Poets* (FSG, 2012).

JAMES MCMICHAEL was born in Pasadena, California, in 1939 and studied at the University of California, Santa Barbara, and at Stanford. His first collection of poems, *Against the Falling Evil*, was published in 1971, and was followed by *The Lover's Familiar* (1978) and *Four Good Things* (1980). *The World at Large: New and Selected Poems, 1971–1996*, appeared in 1996. He teaches at the University of California, Irvine.

McMichael's collections published by FSG are *Capacity* (2006) and *If You Can Tell* (2016).

JOSHUA MEHIGAN was born in 1969 in upstate New York and received an MFA from Sarah Lawrence College. His first full-length book of poems, *The Optimist*, appeared in 2004.

FSG published his second book, *Accepting the Disaster*, in 2014.

IMAN MERSAL was born near Mansoura, Egypt, in 1966 and lives in Alberta, Canada. Her first book of poems in English translation, *These Are Not Oranges, My Love*, was published in 2008. She is a professor of Arabic language and literature at the University of Alberta.

FSG will publish *The Threshold*, translated by Robyn Creswell, in 2022.

ANGE MLINKO was born in Philadelphia in 1969 and received an MFA from Brown University. Her first collection of poems, *Matinées*, was published in 1999. She teaches at the University of Florida.

FSG has published two of her books: *Marvelous Things Overheard* (2013) and *Distant Mandate* (2017). A third collection, *Venice*, will appear in 2022.

EUGENIO MONTALE was born in Genoa, Italy, on October 12, 1896. He trained as an opera singer before turning to poetry and published his first collection, *Ossi di seppia* (*Cuttlefish Bones*), in 1925. Other significant early collections include *Le occasioni* (*The Occasions*) (1939) and *La bufera e altro* (*The Storm and Other Poems*) (1956), which was translated into English in 1978 by Charles Wright, followed by five other collections of late work. Montale was awarded the Nobel Prize in Literature in 1975 and died in Milan on September 12, 1981.

Montale's many translators into English include Robert Lowell (in *Imitations*), William Arrowsmith, and Jonathan Galassi, whose version of his *Collected Poems 1920–1954* was published by FSG in 1998. A translation of his later poetry is forthcoming.

MARIANNE MOORE was born in Kirkwood, Missouri, on November 15, 1887. She graduated from Bryn Mawr College in 1909 and moved to New York City in 1918. Her first book, *Poems*, was published in 1921 under the auspices of the poet H.D., and her second, *Observations*, appeared in 1924. Her first *Selected Poems* was published in 1935 with an introduction by T. S. Eliot. Her *Collected Poems* (1951) received both the Pulitzer Prize and the National Book Award. She died in New York City on February 5, 1972.

In 2016, FSG published a new edition of Moore's *Observations*, edited and introduced by Linda Leavell, followed by the *New Collected Poems* (2017), edited by Heather Cass White. Leavell's biography of Moore, *Holding On Upside Down*, was published by FSG in 2013.

VINÍCIUS DE MORAES was born in Rio de Janeiro on October 19, 1913. He studied law in Brazil and English literature at the University of Oxford, and published his first collection of poems, *O caminho para a distância* (Path into the Distance), in 1933. He became a close friend of Elizabeth Bishop during her stay in Brazil, and she included her translation of Moraes's "Sonnet of Intimacy" in *An Anthology of Twentieth-Century Brazilian Poetry*. A lyricist as well as a poet, Moraes later became known for his collaborations with Antônio Carlos Jobim. He died in Rio on July 9, 1980.

SINÉAD MORRISSEY was born in County Armagh, Northern Ireland, in 1972. She studied at Trinity College, Dublin, and published her first book of poems, *There Was Fire in Vancouver*, in 1996.

In 2015, FSG published her fifth collection, *Parallax*.

VALZHYNA MORT was born in Minsk in 1981. Her first book of poems, *I'm as Thin as Your Eyelashes*, was published in Belarus in 2005, and her U.S. debut, *Factory of Tears*, appeared in 2008.

FSG published *Music for the Dead and Resurrected*, a collection of poems written in English, in 2020. She lives in Ithaca, New York, and teaches at Cornell University.

PAUL MULDOON was born in County Armagh, Northern Ireland, in 1951. He studied at Queen's University Belfast, where he met Seamus Heaney and wrote his first full-length book of poems, *New Weather* (Faber and Faber, 1973). Other significant early works include *Mules* (1977), *Why Brownlee Left* (1980), and *Quoof* (1983).

Collections of his poems published by FSG include *Madoc: A Mystery* (1991), *Selected Poems, 1968–1986* (1993), *The Annals of Chile* (1994), *Hay* (1998), *Poems 1968–1998* (2001), *Moy Sand and Gravel* (2002, recipient of the Pulitzer Prize for Poetry), *Horse Latitudes* (2006), *Maggot* (2010), *The Word on the Street* (2013), *One Thousand Things Worth Knowing* (2015), *Selected Poems 1968–2014* (2016), *Frolic and Detour* (2019), and *Howdie-Skelp* (2021). FSG also published *The End of the Poem* (2006), which gathers his lectures as Professor of Poetry at Oxford from 1999 to 2004. A new collection of essays, *The Eternity of the Poem*, is forthcoming. Muldoon lives in New York City and teaches in Princeton, New Jersey.

LES MURRAY was born in Nabiac, New South Wales, on October 17, 1938, and grew up in neighboring Bunyah. He entered the University of Sydney in 1957 and published *The Weatherboard Cathedral*, his first book of poems under his own name, in 1969.

His first book to be published by FSG, *The Rabbiter's Bounty: Collected Poems*, appeared in 1991. Subsequent collections published by FSG include *Dog Fox Field* (1993), *Translations from the Natural World* (1994), *Subhuman Redneck Poems* (1997, winner of the T. S. Eliot Prize), *Learning Human: New Selected Poems* (2000), *Conscious and Verbal* (2001), *Poems the Size of Photographs* (2003), *The Biplane Houses* (2007), *Taller When Prone* (2011), *New Selected Poems* (2014), and *Waiting for the Past* (2016). Murray is also the author of the verse novels *The Boys Who Stole the Funeral* (1979; FSG edition, 1992) and *Fredy Neptune* (FSG, 1999), as well as *Killing the*

Black Dog: A Memoir of Depression (FSG, 2011). He died on April 29, 2019, in Taree, New South Wales. A posthumous volume of his poems, *Continuous Creation*, will be published in 2022, and a *Collected Poems* is forthcoming.

DANIEL NADLER was born in Toronto in 1983 and received a PhD from Harvard University. FSG published his debut collection, *Lacunae*, in 2016.

PABLO NERUDA was born Ricardo Eliécer Neftalí Reyes Basoalto in Parral, Chile, on July 12, 1904. He moved to Santiago in 1921 to study at the University of Chile and published his first book of poems, *Crepusculario*, in 1923. His most significant early work, *Veinte poemas de amor y una canción desesperada* (*Twenty Love Poems and a Song of Despair*), followed the next year. He entered the diplomatic service in 1927 and spent the next twenty years writing the three volumes of *Residencia en la tierra* (*Residence on Earth*), which appeared between 1933 and 1947. A staunch defender of the Spanish Republic, Neruda would remain a communist for the rest of his life, giving expression to his political philosophy in his *Canto General* (1950). He lived in exile from 1949 to 1953, and wrote numerous books of poems after his return to Chile, including *Odas elementales* (*Elemental Odes*) (1954) and *Cien sonetos de amor* (*One Hundred Love Sonnets*) (1959). He supported Salvador Allende's candidacy for president of Chile in 1970 and was appointed ambassador to France that year. In 1971, Neruda was awarded the Nobel Prize in Literature. He died in Santiago twelve days after Allende's suicide, on September 23, 1973.

Neruda was first published by FSG in 1967, with the appearance of *The Heights of Macchu Picchu*, translated by Nathaniel Tarn. Subsequent books published by FSG include *The Splendor and Death of Joaquin Murieta*, translated by Ben Belitt (1972); *Toward the Splendid City* (1974), Neruda's Nobel lecture; *Extravagaria*, translated by Alastair Reid (1974); *Fully Empowered*, translated by Reid (1975); the *Memoirs*, translated by Hardie St. Martin (1977); *Isla Negra*, translated by Reid (1981); and *Passions and Impressions*, edited by Matilde Urrutia and translated by Margaret Sayers Peden (1982). In 2003, FSG published *The Poetry of Pablo Neruda*, followed by *I Explain a Few Things* in 2007 and *All the Odes* in 2013, all edited by Ilan Stavans. *The Complete Memoirs*, with newly added material translated by Adrian Nathan West, appeared in 2021.

HEBERTO PADILLA was born in Pinar del Río Province, Cuba, on January 20, 1932. His first book of poems, *Las rosas audaces* (The audacious roses), was published in 1948. He was imprisoned by the Castro regime in 1971, and left Cuba in 1980.

Legacies: Selected Poems, translated by Alastair Reid, was published by FSG in 1982. Other books published by FSG include *Heroes Are Grazing in My Garden* (1984), an autobiographical novel; the memoir *Self-Portrait of the Other* (1990); and the poetry collection *A Fountain, a House of Stone* (1991), translated by Reid and Alexander Coleman. Padilla died in Auburn, Alabama, on September 25, 2000.

GRACE PALEY was born on December 11, 1922, in the Bronx, New York. Her first collection of stories, *The Little Disturbances of Man*, appeared in 1959, and her second, *Enormous Changes at the Last Minute*, was published by FSG in 1974. Her third collection, *Later the Same Day*, was published by FSG in 1985; the stories from these three books were republished by FSG in 1994 as *The Collected Stories*. Paley also authored several books of poems, including *Leaning Forward* (1985) and *Begin Again: Collected Poems* (FSG, 2000), as well as a collection of prose, *Just As I Thought* (1998). She died in Thetford, Vermont, on August 22, 2007. Her final book, the poetry collection *Fidelity*, was published by FSG in 2008. *A Grace Paley Reader*, edited by Kevin Bowen and Nora Paley and introduced by George Saunders, was published by FSG in 2017. A biography by Avi Steinberg is forthcoming.

PIER PAOLO PASOLINI was born in Bologna on March 5, 1922. He studied at the University of Bologna and published *Poesie a Casarsa*, a collection of poems written in Friulian, in 1942. He moved to Rome in 1950, where he wrote a series of controversial novels and made his first film, *Accattone* (1961). He published more than ten books of poetry over the course of his life, among them *Le ceneri di Gramsci* (The ashes of Gramsci) (1957) as well as influential works of polemical cultural criticism. He was murdered on November 2, 1975, in Ostia.

In 1996, FSG published Pasolini's *Poems*, selected and translated by Norman MacAfee and Luciano Martinengo.

DON PATERSON was born in Dundee, Scotland, in 1963. His first collection of poems, *Nil Nil*, was published by Faber and Faber in 1993. He teaches at the University of St. Andrews and is the poetry editor for Picador in London. FSG published his collections *Rain* (2010) and *40 Sonnets* (2017).

KATIE PETERSON was born in Menlo Park, California, in 1974. She studied at Stanford and Harvard and published her debut collection of poems, *This One Tree*, in 2006. *A Piece of Good News* was published by FSG in 2019. She edited Robert Lowell's *New Selected Poems* (2017).

CARL PHILLIPS was born in Everett, Washington, in 1959 and studied at Harvard College, the University of Massachusetts Amherst, and Boston University. His first collection of poems, *In the Blood*, appeared in 1992, and his second, *Cortège*, in 1995.

FSG published his fifth book of poems, *The Tether*, in 2001; his subsequent collections, all published by FSG, include *Rock Harbor* (2002), *The Rest of Love* (2004), *Riding Westward* (2006), *Quiver of Arrows: Selected Poems, 1986–2006* (2007), *Speak Low* (2009), *Double Shadow* (2011), *Silverchest* (2013), *Reconnaissance* (2015), *Wild Is the Wind* (2018), and *Pale Colors in a Tall Field* (2020). A new book, *Then the War*, will appear in 2022.

ROWAN RICARDO PHILLIPS was born in New York City in 1974 and received a BA from Swarthmore College and a PhD from Brown University. He is the author of three collections of poems, all published by FSG—*The Ground* (2012), *Heaven* (2015), and *Living Weapon* (2020)—as well as *The Circuit: A Tennis Odyssey* (2018). He teaches at Williams College.

ROBERT PINSKY was born in Long Branch, New Jersey, in 1940 and studied at Rutgers University and Stanford. His first collection of poems, *Sadness and Happiness*, was published in 1975 and was followed by *An Explanation of America* in 1979. He served as the U.S. Poet Laureate from 1997 to 2000 and teaches at Boston University.

Collections published by FSG include *The Figured Wheel: New and Collected Poems, 1966–1996* (1996), *History of My Heart* (1984; first FSG edition, 1997), *Jersey Rain* (2000), *Gulf Music* (2007), *Selected Poems* (2011), and *At the Foundling Hospital* (2016), as well as the nonfiction work *The Sounds of Poetry* (1998). FSG also published his verse translation of Dante's *Inferno* (1994).

JIM POWELL was born in Berkeley, California, in 1951. He published his first book of poems, *It Was Fever That Made the World*, in 1989. In 1993, FSG published *Sappho: A Garland*, a collection of his translations of Sappho.

SALVATORE QUASIMODO was born in Modica, Sicily, on August 20, 1901. He studied civil engineering and worked a variety of jobs before publishing his first books of poems, *Acque e terre* (Waters and lands), in 1930. Following the publication of *Poesie* in 1938 he resigned from his government post and devoted himself to writing. He became involved in the anti-fascist movement during World War II, and several of his later collections testify to his political engagement, among them *Giorno dopo giorno* (Day after day) (1947), *La vita non è sogno* (Life is not a dream) (1949), and *La terra impareggiabile* (Incomparable earth) (1958). He also translated the work of Shakespeare, Neruda, and E. E. Cummings, among others, into Italian. He was awarded the Nobel Prize in Literature in 1959. Quasimodo died in Naples on June 14, 1968.

His *Selected Writings*, edited and translated by Allen Mandelbaum were published by Farrar, Straus and Cudahy in 1960.

SPENCER REECE was born in Hartford, Connecticut, in 1963. He graduated from Wesleyan University in 1985 and published his first book of poems, *The Clerk's Tale*, in 2004.

FSG published his second collection, *The Road to Emmaus*, in 2014. Reece was ordained in the Episcopal Church in 2011 and is priest-in-charge of St. Mark's Church in Jackson Heights, Queens. His new collection, *Acts*, will be published by FSG in 2024.

CHRISTOPHER REID was born in Hong Kong in 1949. He studied at Exeter College, Oxford, and published his first book of poems, *Arcadia*, in 1979. He was poetry editor of Faber and Faber from 1991 to 1999.

FSG published two of his subsequent collections under the title *A Scattering and Anniversary* in 2017. Reid edited the *Letters of Ted Hughes* (2008) and Christopher Logue's *War Music* (2016) and is editing the letters of Seamus Heaney for publication by FSG.

RAINER MARIA RILKE was born in Prague on December 4, 1875. *Leben und Lieder* (Life and songs), his first book of poems, appeared in 1894. His significant poetic works include *Das Stunden-Buch* (*The Book of Hours*) (1905), *Neue Gedichte* (*New Poems*) (1907), and the *Duineser Elegien* (*Duino Elegies*) and *Die Sonette an Orpheus* (*Sonnets to Orpheus*) (both published 1923). Rilke died in Montreux on December 29, 1926.

North Point Press has published much of Rilke's poetry in translations by Edward Snow: *New Poems, 1907* (1982), *New Poems, 1908: The Other Part* (1987), *The Book of Images* (1991), *Uncollected Poems* (1996), the *Duino Elegies* (2000), and *Sonnets to Orpheus* (2004). *The Poetry of Rilke*, translated by Snow and introduced by Adam Zagajewski, was published by North Point in 2009.

ROBIN ROBERTSON was born in Perthshire, Scotland, in 1955 and studied at the University of Aberdeen. *A Painted Field*, his debut collection of verse, appeared in 1997, followed by *Slow Air* (2002) and *Swithering* (2006). He lives in London.

FSG published Robertson's translations of Tomas Tranströmer under the title *The Deleted World* in 2011. *Sailing the Forest: Selected Poems* was published by FSG in 2014.

NELLY SACHS was born in Berlin on December 10, 1891. She fled to Sweden from Nazi Germany in 1940 and became a citizen of the country in 1952. Though she had been writing poetry for many years, her first collection of verse, *In den Wohnungen des Todes* (In the house of death), was not published until 1947. She was awarded the Nobel Prize in Literature in 1966.

Her first book to appear in English, a selection of her poems paired with a verse play, *Eli*, was translated by Michael Hamburger, Michael Roloff, and others and published by FSG in 1967 under the title *O the Chimneys*. A second volume, *The Seeker and Other Poems* (1970) brought together the rest of her work. Sachs died in Stockholm on May 12, 1970. *Flight and Metamorphosis* (2022) is a new translation by Joshua Weiner of one of her most significant collections.

GJERTRUD SCHNACKENBERG was born in Tacoma, Washington, in 1953. She attended Mount Holyoke College and published her first book, *Portraits and Elegies*, in 1982. Her subsequent collections, all published by FSG, are *The Lamplit Answer*

(1985), *A Gilded Lapse of Time* (1992), *The Throne of Labdacus* (2000), *Supernatural Love: Poems, 1976–1992* (2000), and *Heavenly Questions* (2010). She lives in Boston.

JAMES SCHUYLER was born in Chicago on November 9, 1923. He met W. H. Auden while living in New York in the 1940s and served as his secretary on the island of Ischia from 1947 to 1949. He later returned to New York where he befriended John Ashbery and Frank O'Hara. *Freely Espousing*, his first significant collection of verse, was published in 1969. Other collections include *The Crystal Lithium* (1972), *Hymn to Life* (1974), and *The Morning of the Poem* (1980), the first of Schuyler's books to be published by FSG and the recipient of the Pulitzer Prize for Poetry. His *Selected Poems* was published by FSG in 1988. He died in Manhattan on April 12, 1991. In 1993, FSG published his *Collected Poems*, followed by *Other Flowers: Uncollected Poems* in 2010. Nathan Kernan is completing a biography.

DELMORE SCHWARTZ was born in Brooklyn on December 8, 1913. He received a BA from New York University and studied for a time at Harvard. His story "In Dreams Begin Responsibilities" appeared in the first issue of *Partisan Review* in 1937 and was republished in a book of the same name in 1938. His other books include *Vaudeville for a Princess and Other Poems* (1950) and *Summer Knowledge: New and Selected Poems* (1959). He died in New York City on July 11, 1966. James Atlas's biography, *Delmore Schwartz: The Life of an American Poet*, was published by FSG in 1977. In 1986, FSG published *Portrait of Delmore: Journals and Notes*, edited by Elizabeth Pollet. *The Collected Poems of Delmore Schwartz*, edited by Ben Mazer, will be published by FSG in 2023.

CHET'LA SEBREE was born in Chester, Pennsylvania, in 1988. She received an MFA from American University and currently teaches at Bucknell University. Her debut collection, *Mistress*, was published in 2019. Her second collection, *Field Study*, was published by FSG in 2021.

FREDERICK SEIDEL was born in Saint Louis in 1936 and graduated from Harvard College in 1957. His first book of poems, *Final Solutions*, was published by Random House in 1963. His second collection, *Sunrise*, was published in 1980 and received a National Book Critics Circle Award. *My Tokyo*, Seidel's first collection to be published by FSG, appeared in 1993. His subsequent books are *Going Fast* (1998); *The Cosmos Poems* (2000), *Life on Earth* (2001), and *Area Code 212* (2002), which were collected and published under the title *The Cosmos Trilogy* in 2003; *Ooga-Booga* (2006); *Evening Man* (2008); *Poems, 1959–2009* (2009); *Nice Weather* (2012); *Widening Income Inequality* (2016); *Peaches Goes It Alone* (2018); and a selected poems, *Frederick Seidel Selected* (2020). He lives in Manhattan.

BRENDA SHAUGHNESSY was born in Okinawa in 1970 and received an MFA from Columbia University. Her debut collection, *Interior with Sudden Joy*, was published by FSG in 1999. She is the author of four subsequent volumes of poetry and teaches at Rutgers University–Newark.

STEVIE SMITH was born Florence Margaret Smith in Hull, Yorkshire, on September 20, 1902. She moved with her family to North London at the age of three, where she would spend much of the rest of her life. Smith worked as a secretary at a publishing house, a job that inspired her first work of fiction, *Novel on Yellow Paper* (1936). Her first collection of poems, *A Good Time Was Had By All*, appeared in 1937, and was followed by eight more collections in her lifetime, including *Not Waving but Drowning* (1957). Smith died in Ashburton, Devon, on March 7, 1971.

In 1982, FSG published *Me Again: Uncollected Writings of Stevie Smith.*

KAREN SOLIE was born in Moose Jaw, Saskatchewan, in 1966 and studied at the University of Lethbridge and University of Victoria. Her first book of poems, *Short Haul Engine*, was published in 2001, followed by *Modern and Normal* (2005) and *Pigeon* (2009). Two of her collections have been published by FSG: *The Road In Is Not the Same Road Out* (2015) and *The Caiplie Caves* (2020).

ALEKSANDR SOLZHENITSYN was born in Kislovodsk, Russian SFSR, on December 11, 1918. He studied mathematics and physics at Rostov State University and served in the Red Army during World War II before being sentenced to eight years in Soviet labor camps, where he composed and memorized the poems *The Trail* and *Prussian Nights*. He was exonerated in the wake of Khrushchev's Secret Speech and published his only major book to appear in the USSR, the novel *One Day in the Life of Ivan Denisovich*, in 1962. He was awarded the 1970 Nobel Prize in Literature, which he accepted in 1974 after his expulsion from the Soviet Union following the 1973 publication of *The Gulag Archipelago*. He settled in the United States before returning to Russia in 1994, where he died in Moscow on August 3, 2008.

Among Solzhenitsyn's many books published by FSG are *Cancer Ward* (1969, trans. Nicholas Bethell and David Burg), *Stories and Prose Poems* (1971, trans. Michael Glenny), *One Day in the Life of Ivan Denisovich* (1971, trans. H. T. Willetts), *August 1914* (1972, trans. Willetts), and *Prussian Nights* (1977, trans. Robert Conquest).

A. E. STALLINGS was born in Decatur, Georgia, in 1968 and studied at the University of Georgia and Lady Margaret Hall, Oxford. Her debut collection, *Archaic Smile*, was published in 1999, followed by *Hapax* (2006) and *Olives* (2012). In 2018, FSG published her fourth collection of poetry, *Like*. Her *Selected Poems* and a new edition of *Archaic Smile* are forthcoming. She lives in Athens, Greece.

HANNAH SULLIVAN was born in London in 1979. She studied at Trinity College, Cambridge, and Harvard and published her first collection of verse, *Three Poems*, in 2018. It received the T. S. Eliot Prize and was published in the United States by FSG in 2020. She lives in London.

ALLEN TATE was born in Winchester, Kentucky, on November 19, 1899. He studied at Vanderbilt University, where he became associated with the Fugitives, and published his first book of verse, *Mr. Pope and Other Poems*, in 1928. As a teacher, he influenced a number of poets including Theodore Roethke, John Berryman, and Robert Lowell, who would go on to be a lifelong friend. In 1977, FSG published Tate's *Collected Poems: 1919–1976*. He died in Nashville on February 9, 1979.

TOMAS TRANSTRÖMER was born in Stockholm on April 15, 1931. He studied psychology at Stockholm University and published his debut collection, *17 dikter* (17 poems), in 1954. Other important works include the long poem *Östersjöar* (*Baltics*) (1974), *För levande och döda* (*For the Living and the Dead*) (1989), and *Sorgegondolen* (*The Sorrow Gondola*) (1996). He was awarded the Nobel Prize in Literature in 2011; that year, FSG published *The Deleted World: Poems*, with translations by Robin Robertson. He died in Stockholm on March 26, 2015.

CHASE TWICHELL was born in New Haven, Connecticut, in 1950. She received an MFA from the Iowa Writers' Workshop and published her first book of poems, *Northern Spy*, in 1981. FSG published her third collection, *Perdido*, in 1991.

GIUSEPPE UNGARETTI was born in Alexandria, Egypt, on February 8, 1888. He moved to Paris in 1912, where he studied at the Sorbonne, before serving on the Italian front in World War I. He wrote his first book of poems, *Il porto sepolto* (The buried port) (1916), while still a soldier. His other important collections include *Allegria di naufragi* (Joy of shipwrecks) (1919), *Sentimento del tempo* (The feeling of time) (1933), and *Il dolore* (*Pain*) (1947). He died in Milan on June 2, 1970.

FSG published Ungaretti's *Selected Poems*, translated by Andrew Frisardi, in 2002.

JEAN VALENTINE was born in Chicago on April 27, 1934, and raised in California. She was educated at Milton Academy and graduated from Radcliffe in 1956. Her first book, *Dream Barker, and Other Poems* (1965), was awarded the Yale Younger Poets prize. FSG published her next three collections of verse: *Pilgrims* (1969), *Ordinary Things* (1974), and *The Messenger* (1979). *Door in the Mountain: New and Collected Poems, 1965–2003* (Wesleyan University Press, 2004) received the National Book Award. She died in New York City on December 29, 2020.

PAUL VALÉRY was born in Sète, France, on October 30, 1871, and raised in Montpellier. He began publishing as a young man, but his first major poetic work, *La*

Jeune Parque (The young Fate), appeared in 1917 after a prolonged period of silence following the death of his mentor Stéphane Mallarmé. He published two more small volumes of poems, *Album des vers anciens* (Album of old verse) (1920) and *Charmes* (1922), which included the poem "Le Cimitière marin." He spent his later years writing prose and assembling his monumental *Cahiers*. He died in Paris on July 20, 1945.

In 2020, FSG published *The Idea of Perfection*, a bilingual selection of Valéry's poetry and prose, edited and translated by Nathaniel Rudavsky-Brody.

DEREK WALCOTT was born in Castries, Saint Lucia, on January 23, 1930. He published his first poem in a Saint Lucian newspaper at age fourteen, and in 1948 he self-published his first chapbook, *25 Poems*. He studied at the University College of the West Indies in Kingston before moving to Trinidad, and published his first significant collection of verse, *In a Green Night: Poems, 1948–60*, in 1962. In 1964, a *Selected Poems* was published by Farrar, Straus and Company. His major works, all published by FSG, are *The Gulf and Other Poems* (1970), *Another Life* (1973), *Sea Grapes* (1976), *The Star-Apple Kingdom* (1979), *The Fortunate Traveller* (1982), *Midsummer* (1984), *Collected Poems, 1948–1984* (1986), *The Arkansas Testament* (1987), the epic poem *Omeros* (1990), *The Bounty* (1997), *Tiepolo's Hound* (2000), *The Prodigal* (2004), a new *Selected Poems* edited by Edward Baugh (2007), *White Egrets* (2010), *The Poetry of Derek Walcott 1948–2013* (2014), and *Morning, Paramin* (2016).

FSG has also published Walcott's dramatic works, including *Dream on Monkey Mountain and Other Plays* (1971), *The Joker of Seville and O Babylon!* (1978), *Remembrance and Pantomime* (1980), *Three Plays: The Last Carnival; Beef, no Chicken; and A Branch of the Blue Nile* (1986), *Capeman* (1997), *The Haitian Trilogy: Henri Christophe, Drums and Colours, and The Haitian Earth* (2002), *Walker and the Ghost Dance* (2002), *Moon-Child* (2011), and *O Starry Starry Night* (2014), as well as the nonfiction work with Joseph Brodsky and Seamus Heaney, *Homage to Robert Frost* (1996), and the essay collection *What the Twilight Says* (1998). In 1992, Walcott was awarded the Nobel Prize in Literature. He died in Gros Islet, Saint Lucia, on March 17, 2017. An edition of his collected prose is being prepared by Christian Campbell.

SUSAN WHEELER was born in Pittsburgh in 1955. *Bag 'o' Diamonds*, her debut collection, appeared in 1993. Among her other books are *Smokes* (1998), *Ledger* (2005), and *Meme* (2012). She teaches at Princeton. In 2009, FSG published her *Assorted Poems*.

C. K. WILLIAMS was born in Newark, New Jersey, on December 4, 1936. He studied at Bucknell and the University of Pennsylvania and published his first full-length book, *Lies*, in 1969, followed by *I Am the Bitter Name* (1972), *With Ignorance* (1977), and *Tar* (1983).

Flesh and Blood (1987), his first collection to be published by FSG, received the National Book Critics Circle Award for poetry. His subsequent major collections, all published by FSG, are *Poems, 1963–1983* (1988), *A Dream of Mind* (1992), *Selected Poems* (1994), *The Vigil* (1997), *Repair* (1999, winner of the Pulitzer Prize), *The Singing* (2003, winner of the National Book Award), *Collected Poems* (2006), *Wait* (2010), *Writers Writing Dying* (2012), *All at Once* (2014), *Selected Later Poems* (2015), and the posthumous *Falling Ill: Last Poems* (2017). FSG also published his translation of Euripides's *The Bacchae* (1990) and his memoir *Misgivings: My Mother, My Father, Myself* (2000). He died in Hopewell, New Jersey, on September 20, 2015. A new selection of his work is forthcoming.

CHRISTIAN WIMAN was born in 1966 in West Texas. He attended Washington and Lee University and published his first book of poems, *The Long Home*, in 1998. His collections published by FSG are *Every Riven Thing* (2010), *Once in the West* (2014), *Hammer Is the Prayer* (2016), and *Survival Is a Style* (2020). FSG also published his nonfiction works *My Bright Abyss* (2013) and *He Held Radical Light* (2018). He is currently preparing an anthology, *Fifty Entries Against Despair*, to be published in 2022. Wiman was the editor of *Poetry* magazine from 2003 to 2013 and now teaches at Yale University.

CHARLES WRIGHT was born in Pickwick Dam, Tennessee, in 1935 and attended Davidson College. He served in the army in Italy, an experience that would influence much of his poetry, and later received an MFA from the Iowa Writers' Workshop. His early books of poems include *The Grave of the Right Hand* (1970), *Hard Freight* (1973), *Bloodlines* (1975), and *China Trace* (1977), as well as *The Storm and Other Poems* (1978), a collection of his translations of Eugenio Montale. *Country Music: Selected Early Poems* (1982) received the National Book Award. He taught for many years at the University of California, Irvine, and the University of Virginia and served as U.S. Poet Laureate from 2014 to 2015.

Wright's collections published by FSG are *Zone Journals* (1988), *The World of Ten Thousand Things* (1990), *Chickamauga* (1995), the Pulitzer Prize–winning *Black Zodiac* (1997), *Appalachia* (1998), *Negative Blue: Selected Later Poems* (2000), *A Short History of the Shadow* (2002), *Buffalo Yoga* (2004), *Scar Tissue* (2006), *Littlefoot: A Poem* (2007), *Sestets* (2009), *Bye-and-Bye: Selected Late Poems* (2011), *Caribou* (2014), and a career-spanning collection, *Oblivion Banjo: The Poetry of Charles Wright* (2019).

JAMES WRIGHT was born in Martins Ferry, Ohio, on December 13, 1927. He attended Kenyon College after serving in the army in Japan, graduating in 1952. His debut collection, *The Green Wall* (1957), received the Yale Younger Poets prize. *The Branch Will Not Break*, widely considered his poetic breakthrough, appeared in 1963, and his *Collected Poems* (1971) was awarded the Pulitzer Prize.

FSG published *Two Citizens* in 1973, followed by *To a Blossoming Pear Tree* in 1977. He died in New York City on March 25, 1980. In 1990, FSG copublished *Above the River: The Complete Poems* with Wesleyan University Press. A new *Selected Poems*, edited by Robert Bly and Anne Wright, appeared in 2005 along with *A Wild Perfection: The Selected Letters of James Wright*, edited by Anne Wright and Saundra Maley. Wright also translated Hermann Hesse's *Selected Poems*, published by FSG in 1970. Jonathan Blunk's biography, *James Wright: A Life in Poetry*, was published by FSG in 2017.

DAVID YOUNG was born in Davenport, Iowa, in 1936. He studied at Carleton College and Yale and published his first book of poems, *Sweating Out the Winter*, in 1969. Young taught for many years at Oberlin, where he edited the magazine *Field*. He translated *The Poetry of Petrarch* (FSG, 2004).

ADAM ZAGAJEWSKI was born in Lvov, Ukranian SSR, in 1945 and was forcibly relocated with his family to Poland that year. His first collection of verse in English translation, *Tremor*, was published by FSG in 1985. Subsequent collections of poetry in English, all published by FSG, include *Canvas* (1991), *Mysticism for Beginners* (1999), *Without End* (2002), *Eternal Enemies* (2008), *Unseen Hand* (2011), and *Asymmetry* (2018), as well as the essay collections *Two Cities* (1995), *Another Beauty* (2000), *A Defense of Ardor* (2004), and *Slight Exaggeration* (2017). Zagajewski's translators include Clare Cavanagh, Renata Gorczynski, Benjamin Ivry, and C. K. Williams. A new collection, *True Life*, translated by Clare Cavanagh, will be published in 2022, to be followed by *Collected Poems*, also edited by Clare Cavanagh. He died in Kraków on March 21, 2021.

Acknowledgments

Our thanks, first of all, to the poets and translators, and the editors and publishers, who contributed to the creation and realization of this anthology.

We would also like to express appreciation to those who helped shape the FSG poetry list over the years, especially Michael Roloff, Michael Di Capua, Pat Strachan, David Rieff, Helen Graves, Jane Bobko, Ann Kjellberg, Carmen Gomezplata, Lynn Warshow, John Glusman, Paul Elie, Lorin Stein, Mitzi Angel, Sean MacDonald, Jackson Howard, and Daniel Vazquez.

Our gratitude also goes to Katharine Liptak, Ian Van Wye, Erika Seidman, Debra Helfand, Brianna Panzica, Logan Hill, Na Kim, Andrew Mandel, Eric Chinski, and especially Mitzi, who were instrumental in making this book into a book.

Index of Authors, Titles, and First Lines

Authors and translators are in SMALL CAPS.
Titles are in *italics*.
First lines are in plain text.

Sources and Permissions

Yehuda Amichai, from *Time*, copyright © 1978 by Yehuda Amichai, Harper & Row, 1978. Translation copyright © 1978 by Ted Hughes. Published by FSG in 2015 in *The Poetry of Yehuda Amichai*.

John Ashbery, "The Problem of Anxiety," from *Can You Hear, Bird*, copyright © 1995 by John Ashbery. Reprinted by permission of Georges Borchardt, Inc. for the author's Estate. Published by FSG in 1995 in *Can You Hear, Bird*.

John Ashbery, "Real Time," from *Chinese Whispers*, copyright © 2002 by John Ashbery. Reprinted by permission of Georges Borchardt, Inc. for the author's Estate. Published by FSG in 2002 in *Chinese Whispers*.

Ingeborg Bachmann, "Autumn Maneuver" or "Herbstmanöver" from *Werke Band I*, copyright © 1978 by Piper Verlag GmGH, München/Berlin. Translated copyright © 1994 by Peter Filkins, from *Songs in Flight: The Complete Poetry of Ingeborg Bachmann*. Published by FSG in 2006 in *Twentieth-Century German Poetry: An Anthology*.

Charles Baudelaire, "Meditation," from *Les Fleurs du Mal*. Translation copyright © 2021 by Nathaniel Rudavsky-Brody. To appear in 2025 in *Les Fleurs du Mal*.

Sylvie Baumgartel, "*Cum Clave*," from *Pink*, copyright © 2021 by Sylvie Baumgartel. Published by FSG in 2021 in *Pink*.

Gottfried Benn, "Little Aster," from *Morgue und andere Gedichte*. Translation copyright © 2013 by Michael Hofmann. Published by FSG in 2013 in *Impromptus*.

Charles Bernstein, "A Defence of Poetry," from *All the Whiskey in Heaven*, copyright © 2010 by Charles Bernstein. Published by FSG in 2010 in *All the Whiskey in Heaven*.

John Berryman, "Dream Song #22," "Dream Song #29," "Dream Song #90," and "Dream Song #149," from *77 Dream Songs*, copyright © 1959, 1962, 1963, 1964 by John Berryman. Copyright renewed © 1992 by Kate Donahue Berryman. Published by FSG in 1964 in *77 Dream Songs*.

John Berryman, "Dream Song #90" and "Dream Song #149," from *His Toy, His Dream, His Rest*, copyright © 1968 by John Berryman. Published by FSG in 1968 in *His Toy, His Dream, His Rest*.

John Berryman, "The Ball Poem," from *The Dispossessed*, copyright © 1948 by John Berryman. Published by FSG in 1989 in *John Berryman: Collected Poems 1937–1971*.

John Betjeman, "The Heart of Thomas Hardy," from *Continual Dew*, copyright © 1937 by John Betjeman. Published by FSG in 2006 in *Collected Poems*.

Frank Bidart, "Guilty of Dust," from *In the Western Light*, copyright © 1990 by Frank Bidart. Published by FSG in 1990 in *In the Western Light*.

Frank Bidart, "Half-light," from *Half-light*, copyright © 2017 by Frank Bidart. Published by FSG in 2017 in *Half-light*.

Frank Bidart, "On My Seventy-Eighth," from *Against Silence*, copyright © 2021 by Frank Bidart. Published by FSG in 2021 in *Against Silence*.

Elizabeth Bishop, "Cape Breton," from *North & South—A Cold Spring*, copyright © 1955 by Elizabeth Bishop. Published by FSG in 1983 in *Elizabeth Bishop: The Complete Poems 1927–1979*.

Elizabeth Bishop, "Santarém," from *Elizabeth Bishop: The Complete Poems, 1927–1979*, copyright © 1979, 1983 by Alice Helen Methfessel. Copyright © 1933, 1935, 1936, 1937, 1938, 1939, 1940, 1941, 1944, 1945, 1946, 1947, 1948, 1949, 1951, 1952, 1955, 1956, 1957, 1958, 1959, 1960, 1961, 1962, 1963, 1964, 1965, 1966, 1967, 1968, 1969, 1971, 1972, 1973, 1974, 1975, 1976, 1978 by Elizabeth Bishop. Renewal copyright © 1967, 1968, 1971, 1974, 1974, 1975, 1976, 1979 by Elizabeth Bishop. Copyright renewal © 1980 by Alice Helen Methfessel. Published by FSG in 1983 in *Elizabeth Bishop: The Complete Poems 1927–1979*.

Elizabeth Bishop, "North Haven," from *Elizabeth Bishop: The Complete Poems, 1927–1979*, copyright © 1979, 1983 by Alice Helen Methfessel. Copyright © 1933, 1935, 1936, 1937, 1938, 1939, 1940, 1941, 1944, 1945, 1946, 1947, 1948, 1949, 1951, 1952, 1955, 1956, 1957, 1958, 1959, 1960, 1961, 1962, 1963, 1964, 1965, 1966, 1967, 1968, 1969, 1971, 1972, 1973, 1974, 1975, 1976, 1978 by Elizabeth Bishop. Renewal copyright © 1967, 1968, 1971, 1974, 1974, 1975, 1976, 1979 by Elizabeth Bishop. Copyright renewal © 1980 by Alice Helen Methfessel. Published by FSG in 1983 in *Elizabeth Bishop: The Complete Poems 1927–1979*.

Elizabeth Bishop, "Vague Poem (*Vaguely Love Poem*)," from *Edgar Allan Poe & the Juke-Box*, copyright © 2006 by Alice Helen Methfessel. Published by FSG in 2006 in *Edgar Allan Poe & the Juke-Box*.

Louise Bogan, "Night," from *The Blue Estuaries: Poems, 1923–1968*, copyright © 1968 by Louise Bogan. Published by FSG in 1968 in *The Blue Estuaries: Poems, 1923–1968*.

Yves Bonnefoy, "*Passerby these are words...*" from Yves Bonnefoy, *Les Planches courbes*, copyright © 2001 by Mercure de France. Translation copyright © 2006 by Hoyt Rogers. Published by FSG in 2006 in *The Curved Planks*.

Joseph Brodsky, "To Urania," from *Uraniia,* copyright © 1981, 1982, 1983, 1984, 1985, 1986, 1987, 1988 by Joseph Brodsky. Translation copyright © 1988 by Joseph Brodsky. Published by FSG in 1988 in *To Urania.*

Joseph Brodsky, "A Song," from *So Forth,* copyright © 1996 by Joseph Brodsky. Published by FSG in 1996 in *So Forth.*

Rosellen Brown, from *Cora Fry's Pillow Book,* copyright © 1994 by Rosellen Brown. Published by FSG in 1994 in *Cora Fry's Pillow Book.*

Patrizia Cavalli, "Very simple love that believes in words," from *Pigre divinità e pigra sorte,* copyright © 1974 by Giulio Einaudi Editore, s.p.a., Torino. Translation copyright © 2013 by J. D. McClatchy. Published by FSG in 2013 in *My Poems Won't Change the World.*

Paul Celan, "Answered," from *Die Gedichte,* copyright © 2003 by Suhrkamp Verlag, Berlin. Reprinted by permission of Suhrkamp Verlag, Berlin. Translation copyright © 2014 by Pierre Joris. Published by FSG in 2014 in *Breathturn into Timestead: The Collected Later Poetry.*

Paul Celan, "Psalm," from *Die Niemandsrose,* copyright © 1963 by S. Fischer Verlag GmbH, Frankfurt am Main. Reprinted by permission of Suhrkamp Verlag, Berlin. Translation copyright © 2020 Pierre Joris.

Eleanor Chai, "Thick Description," from *Standing Water,* copyright © 2016 by Eleanor Chai. Published by FSG in 2016 in *Standing Water.*

Po Chü-i, "Crimson-Weave Carpet." Translation copyright © 2008 by David Hinton. Published by FSG in 2008 in *Classical Chinese Poetry: An Anthology.*

John Clare, "The Pettichap's Nest," from *The Rural Muse.* Published by FSG in 2008 in *"I Am": The Selected Poetry of John Clare.*

Jeff Clark, "Blood Dub," from *Music and Suicide,* copyright © 2004 by Jeff Clark. Published by FSG in 2004 in *Music and Suicide.*

Killarney Clary, "Above the Inland Empire today," from *Who Whispered Near Me,* copyright © 1989 by Killarney Clary. Published by FSG in 1989 in *Who Whispered Near Me.*

Leonard Cohen, "Almost Like the Blues," from *The Flame,* copyright © 2018 by Old Ideas, LLC. Published by FSG in 2019 in *The Flame.*

Henri Cole, "Self-Portrait as the Red Princess," from *Middle Earth,* copyright © 2003 by Henri Cole. Published by FSG in 2003 in *Middle Earth.*

Henri Cole, "Self-Portrait with Rifle," from *Nothing to Declare*, copyright © 2015 by Henri Cole. Published by FSG in 2015 in *Nothing to Declare*.

Peter Cole, "Through the Slaughter," from *Hymns & Qualms: New and Selected Poems and Translations*, copyright © 2017 by Peter Cole. Published by FSG in 2017 in *Hymns & Qualms: New and Selected Poems and Translations*.

Averill Curdy, "When I was beautiful," from *Song & Error*, copyright © 2013 by Averill Curdy. Published by FSG in 2013 in *Song & Error*.

Mahmoud Darwish, from "Eleven Planets at the End of the Andalusian Scene," from *Eleven Planets*, copyright © 1992 by Mahmoud Darwish. Translation copyright © 2009 by Fady Joudah. Published by FSG in 2009 in *If I Were Another*.

Lydia Davis, "Trying to Learn," from *Almost No Memory*, copyright © 1997 by Lydia Davis. Published by FSG in 1997 in *Almost No Memory*.

Carlos Drummond de Andrade, "Buried Alive," from *Farmer in the Clouds*, copyright © 1954 by Carlos Drummond de Andrade. Translation copyright © 2015 by Richard Zenith. Published by FSG in 2015 in *Multitudinous Heart*.

Carol Ann Duffy, "Hive," from *Rapture*, copyright © 2005 by Carol Ann Duffy. Published by FSG in 2005 in *Rapture*.

Stuart Dybek, "Election Day," from *Streets in Their Own Ink*, copyright © 2004 by Stuart Dybek. Published by FSG in 2004 in *Streets in Their Own Ink*.

T. S. Eliot, "Marina," from *Collected Poems, 1909–1962* by T. S. Eliot. Copyright © 1930 by T. S. Eliot, renewed 1958 by Thomas Stearns Eliot. Copyright © 1956 by Thomas Stearns Eliot, renewed 1984 by Esme Valerie Eliot. Reprinted by permission of Houghton Mifflin Harcourt Publishing Company. All rights reserved. Published by FSG in 2018 in *The Poems of T. S. Eliot: Volume I*.

T. S. Eliot, "A Dedication to my Wife," from *Collected Poems, 1909–1962* by T. S. Eliot. Copyright © 1930 by T. S. Eliot, renewed 1958 by Thomas Stearns Eliot. Copyright © 1956 by Thomas Stearns Eliot, renewed 1984 by Esme Valerie Eliot. Reprinted by permission of Houghton Mifflin Harcourt Publishing Company. All rights reserved. Published by FSG in 1959 in *The Elder Statesman*, revised 1963.

Luciano Erba, "Vanitas Varietatum," from *Il mane minore*, copyright © 1960 by Luciano Erba. Translation copyright © 2012 by Charles Wright. Published by FSG in 2012 in *The FSG Book of Twentieth-Century Italian Poetry*.

Marie Étienne, from *King of a Hundred Horsemen*, copyright © 2002 by Flammarion. Translation copyright © 2008 by Marilyn Macker. Published by FSG in 2008 in *King of a Hundred Horsemen*.

Durs Grünbein, "Lament of a Legionnaire on Germanicus's Campaign to the Elbe River," from *Nach Den Satiren*, copyright © 1999, 2005 by Durs Grünbein. Translation copyright © 2005 by Michael Hofmann. Published by FSG in 2005 in *Ashes for Breakfast: Selected Poems*.

Thom Gunn, "Rites of Passage," from *Moly*, copyright © 1971 by Thom Gunn. Published by FSG in 1971 in *Moly*.

Thom Gunn, "The Man with Night Sweats," from *The Man with Night Sweats*, copyright © 1992 by Thom Gunn. Published by FSG in 1992 in *The Man with Night Sweats*.

francine j. Harris, "Oregon Trail, Missouri," from *Here is the Sweet Hand*, copyright © 2020 by francine j. harris. Published by FSG in 2020 in *Here is the Sweet Hand*.

Tony Harrison, "Changing at York," from *V. and Other Poems*, copyright © 1989 by Tony Harrison. Published by FSG in 1989 in *V. and Other Poems*.

From *Beowulf*, translation copyright © 2020 by Maria Dahvana Headley. Published by FSG in 2020 in *Beowulf*.

Seamus Heaney, "Oysters," from *Field Work*, copyright © 1976, 1979 by Seamus Heaney. Published by FSG in 1979 in *Field Work*.

Seamus Heaney, "Clearances, III," from *The Haw Lantern*, copyright © 1987 by Seamus Heaney. Published by FSG in 1987 in *The Haw Lantern*.

Seamus Heaney, "Bogland," from *Door into the Dark*, copyright © 1969 by Seamus Heaney. Published by FSG in 1998 in *Opened Ground: Poems, 1966–1996*.

From *Beowulf*, translation copyright © 2000 by Seamus Heaney. Published by FSG in 2000 in *Beowulf*.

Seamus Heaney, "Postscript," from *The Spirit Level*, copyright © 1996 by Seamus Heaney. Published by FSG in 1996 in *The Spirit Level*.

Hermann Hesse, "Ravenna (1)," from *Die Gedichte*, copyright © 1953 by Suhrkamp Verlag. Translation copyright © 1970 by James Wright. Published by FSG in 1970 in *Poems*.

Michael Hofmann, "My Father's House Has Many Mansions," from *Acrimony*, copyright © 1986 by Michael Hofmann. Published by FSG in 2009 in *Selected Poems*.

Richard Howard, "A Lost Art," from *Like Most Revelations*, copyright © 1994 by Richard Howard. Published by FSG in 2004 in *Inner Voices: Selected Poems, 1963–2003*.

Ovid, "Arethusa." Version copyright © 1997 by Ted Hughes. Published by FSG in 1997 in *Tales From Ovid*.

Magrelli. Translation copyright © 2010 by Jamie McKendrick. Published by FSG in 2010 in *Vanishing Points*.

Roya Marsh, "in broad dayliGht black moms look grieving," from *dayliGht*, copyright © 2020 by Roya Marsh. Published by FSG in 2020 in *dayliGht*.

Glyn Maxwell, "The Ginger-Haired in Heaven," from *Rest for the Wicked*, copyright © 1995 by Glyn Maxwell. Published by FSG in 2011 in *One Thousand Nights and Counting: Selected Poems*.

Shane McCrae, "Seawhere," from *The Gilded Auction Block*, copyright © 2019 by Shane McCrae. Published by FSG in 2019 in *The Gilded Auction Block*.

Shane McCrae, "The Butterflies the Mountain and the Lake," from *Cain Named the Animal*. Copyright © 2021 by Shane McCrae. To be published in 2022 in *Cain Named the Animal*.

Maureen N. McLane, "Excursion Susan Sontag," from *Same Life*, copyright © 2008 by Maureen N. McLane. Published by FSG in 2008 in *Same Life*.

Maureen N. McLane, "They Were Not Kidding in the Fourteenth Century," from *This Blue*, copyright © 2014 by Maureen N. McLane. Published by FSG in 2014 in *This Blue*.

James McMichael, "Above the Red Deep-Water Clays," from *Capacity*, copyright © 2006 by James McMichael. Published by FSG in 2006 in *Capacity*.

Joshua Mehigan, "The Smokestack," from *Accepting the Disaster*, copyright © 2014 by Joshua Mehigan. Published by FSG in 2014 in *Accepting the Disaster*.

Iman Mersal, "They tear down my family home," from *Jughrafiya badila*, copyright © 2006 by Iman Mersal. Translation copyright © 2021 by Robyn Creswell. To be published in 2022 in *The Threshold*.

Ange Mlinko, "Gelsenkirchen," from *Distant Mandate*, copyright © 2017 by Ange Mlinko. Published by FSG in 2017 in *Distant Mandate*.

Ange Mlinko, "Venice, Florida," from *Venice*. Copyright © 2021 by Ange Mlinko. To be published in 2022 in *Venice*.

Eugenio Montale, "The Eel" from *Collected Poems 1920–1954*, translated and edited by Jonathan Galassi. Copyright © Mondadori Libri SpA, Milano. Translation copyright © 1998, 2000, 2012 by Jonathan Galassi.

Eugenio Montale, "Bellosguardo" by Eugenio Montale, translated by Robert Lowell from *Collected Poems* by Robert Lowell. Copyright © Mondadori Libri SpA, Milano. Translation copyright © 2003 by Harriet Lowell and Sheridan Lowell.

Eugenio Montale, "The Arno at Rovezzano," from *Satura*, copyright © Modadori Libri SpA, Milano. Translated by Jonathan Galassi.

Marianne Moore, "To a Giraffe," from *The Arctic Ox*, copyright © 1964 by Marianne Moore. Published by FSG in 2017 in *New Collected Poems*.

Sinéad Morrissey, "The Coal Jetty," from *Parallax*, copyright © 2015 by Sinéad Morrissey. Published by FSG in 2015 in *Parallax*.

Valzhyna Mort, "Singer," from *Music for the Dead and Resurrected*, copyright © 2020 by Valzhyna Mort. Published by FSG in 2020 in *Music for the Dead and Resurrected*.

Paul Muldoon, "Milkweed and Monarch," from *The Annals of Chile*, copyright © 1994 by Paul Muldoon. Published by FSG in 1994 in *The Annals of Chile*.

Paul Muldoon, "As," from *Moy Sand and Gravel*, copyright © 2002 by Paul Muldoon. Published by FSG in 2002 in *Moy Sand and Gravel*.

Paul Muldoon, "The Fly," from *Howdie-Skelp*, copyright © 2021 by Paul Muldoon. Published by FSG in 2021 in *Howdie-Skelp*.

Les Murray, "Water-Gardening in an Old Farm Dam," from *Subhuman Redneck Poems*, copyright © 1997 by Les Murray. Published by FSG in 1997 in *Subhuman Redneck Poems*.

Les Murray, "The Dream of Wearing Shorts Forever," from *The Daylight Moon*, copyright © 1987 by Les Murray. Published by FSG in 1991 in *The Rabbiter's Bounty: Collected Poems*.

Daniel Nadler, "Love," from *Lacunae*, copyright © 2016 by Daniel Nadler. Published by FSG in 2016 in *Lacunae*.

Pablo Neruda, "We Are Many" or "Muchos somos," from *Extravagario*, copyright © 1958 by Pablo Neruda and Fundación Pablo Neruda. Translation copyright © 1974 by Alastair Reid. Published by FSG in 1974 in *Extravagaria*.

Pablo Neruda, "Ode to a Pair of Socks" or "Oda a los calcetines," from *Nuevas odas elementales*, copyright © 1956 by Pablo Neruda and Fundación Pablo Neruda. Translation copyright © by Mark Strand. Published by FSG in 2003 in *The Poetry of Pablo Neruda*.

Heberto Padilla, "Walking," copyright © Heberto Padilla. Translation © by Alastair Reid. Published by FSG in 1982 in *Legacies: Selected Poems*.

Grace Paley, "Here," from *Begin Again: Collected Poems*, copyright © 2000 by Grace Paley. Published by FSG in 2000 in *Begin Again: Collected Poems*.

Pier Paolo Pasolini, "Lines from the Testament," from *Trasumanar e organizzar*, copyright © 1971 by Pier Paolo Pasolini. Translation copyright © 1996 by Norman MacAfee and Luciano Martinengo. Published by FSG in 1996 in *Poems*.

Don Paterson, "Parallax" and "The Poetry," from *Rain*, copyright © 2010 by Don Paterson. Published by FSG in 2010 in *Rain*.

Katie Peterson, "Self Help," from *A Piece of Good News*, copyright © 2019 by Katie Peterson. Published by FSG in 2019 in *A Piece of Good News*.

Petrarch, "My galley loaded with forgetfulness." Translation copyright © 2004 by David Young. Published by FSG in 2004 in *The Poetry of Petrarch*.

Carl Phillips, "Riding Westward," from *Riding Westward*, copyright © 2006 by Carl Phillips. Published by FSG in 2006 in *Riding Westward*.

Carl Phillips, "If You Will, I Will," from *Wild Is the Wind*, copyright © 2018 by Carl Phillips. Published by FSG in 2018 in *Wild Is the Wind*.

Carl Phillips, "Sing a Darkness," from *Then the War*. Copyright © 2021 by Carl Phillips. To be published in 2022 in *Then the War*.

Rowan Ricardo Phillips, "Over the Countries of Kings and Queens Came the Second Idea," from *The Ground*, copyright © 2012 by Rowan Ricardo Phillips. Published by FSG in 2012 in *The Ground*.

Rowan Ricardo Phillips, "Even Homer Nods," from *Living Weapon*, copyright © 2020 by Rowan Ricardo Phillips. Published by FSG in 2020 in *Living Weapon*.

Robert Pinsky, "Shirt," from *The Want Bone*, copyright © 1990 by Robert Pinsky. Published by FSG in 1996 in *The Figured Wheel: New and Collected Poems 1966–1996*.

Sappho, "Artfully adorned Aphrodite, deathless." Translation copyright © 1993 by Jim Powell. Published by FSG in 1993 in *Sappho: A Garland*.

Salvatore Quasimodo, "O My Sweet Animals," from *Giorno dopo giorno*, copyright © 1947 by Salvatore Quasimodo. Translation copyright © 1960 by Allen Mandelbaum. Published by FSG in 1960 in *Selected Writings*.

Spencer Reece, "At Thomas Merton's Grave," from *The Road to Emmaus*, copyright © 2014 by Spencer Reece. Published by FSG in 2014 in *The Road to Emmaus*.

Spencer Reece, "Ephphatha," from *Acts*. Copyright © 2021 by Spencer Reece. To be published in 2024 in *Acts*.

Stevie Smith, "On the Dressing gown lent me by my Hostess the Brazilian Consul in Milan, 1958," from *All the Poems*, copyright © 1937, 1938, 1942, 1950, 1957, 1962, 1966, 1971, 1972 by Stevie Smith. Copyright © 2016 by the Estate of James MacGibbon. Copyright © 2015 by Will May. Reprinted by permission of New Directions Publishing Corp. Published by FSG in 1982 in *Me Again: Uncollected Writings of Stevie Smith*.

Karen Solie, "Affirmations," from *The Road In Is Not the Same Road Out*, copyright © 2015 by Karen Solie. Published by FSG in 2015 in *The Road In Is Not the Same Road Out*.

Aleksandr Solzhenitsyn, from *Prussian Nights*, copyright © 1977 by Aleksandr Solzhenitsyn. Translation copyright © 1977 by Robert Conquest. Published by FSG in 1977 in *Prussian Nights*.

A. E. Stallings, "Empathy," from *Like*, copyright © 2018 by A. E. Stallings. Published by FSG in 2018 in *Like*.

A. E. Stallings, "Apollo Takes Charge of His Muses," from *Archaic Smile*, copyright © 1999 by A. E. Stallings. To be published in 2023 in *Archaic Smile*.

Hannah Sullivan, from "Repeat Until Time," from *Three Poems*, copyright © 2018 by Hannah Sullivan. Published by FSG in 2018 in *Three Poems*.

Allen Tate, from "Seasons of the Soul," from *Poems 1922–1947*, copyright © 1948 by Allen Tate. Published by FSG in 1977 in *Collected Poems: 1919–1976*.

Tomas Tranströmer, "A Winter Night," from *The Deleted World: Poems*, copyright © 2006 by Tomas Tranströmer. Translation copyright © 2006 by Robin Robertson. Published by FSG in 2011 in *The Deleted World: Poems*.

Chase Twichell, "Six Belons," from *Perdido*, copyright © 1991 by Chase Twichell. Published by FSG in 1991 in *Perdido*.

Giuseppe Ungaretti, "Eternal," from *L'Allegria*, copyright © 1931 by Arnoldo Mondadori Editore SpA, Milano. Translation copyright © 2002 by Andrew Frisardi. Published by FSG in 2002 in *Selected Poems*.

Jean Valentine, "Pilgrims," from *Pilgrims*, copyright © 1969 by Jean Valentine. Published by FSG in 1969 in *Pilgrims*.

Paul Valéry, "Pomegranates." Translation copyright © 2020 by Nathaniel Rudavsky-Brody. Published by FSG in 2020 in *The Idea of Perfection*.

Derek Walcott, "Sea Grapes," from *Sea Grapes*, copyright © 1976 by Derek Walcott. Published by FSG in 1976 in *Sea Grapes*.

Derek Walcott, "Gros-Ilet," from *The Arkansas Testament*, copyright © 1987 by Derek Walcott. Published by FSG in 1987 in *The Arkansas Treatment*.

Derek Walcott, "Forty Acres," from *White Egrets*, copyright © 2010 by Derek Walcott. Published by FSG in 2010 in *White Egrets*.

Susan Wheeler, "Loss Leider," from *Ledger*, copyright © 2005 by Susan Wheeler. Published by FSG in 2009 in *Assorted Poems*.

C. K. Williams, "Garden," from *Vigil*, copyright © 1996 by C. K. Williams. Published by FSG in 1996 in *Vigil*.

C. K. Williams, "My Mother's Lips," from *Tar*, copyright © 1983 by C. K. Williams. Published by FSG in 2006 in *Collected Poems*.

Christian Wiman, "From a Window," from *Every Riven Thing*, copyright © 2010 by Christian Wiman. Published by FSG in 2010 in *Every Riven Thing*.

Christian Wiman, "Never Heaven," from *Survival Is a Style*, copyright © 2020 by Christian Wiman. Published by FSG in 2020 in *Survival Is a Style*.

Charles Wright, "The Appalachian Book of the Dead," from *Black Zodiac*, copyright © 1997 by Charles Wright. Published by FSG in 1997 in *Black Zodiac*.

Charles Wright, "Dog Creek Mainline," from *Hard Freight*, copyright © 1973 by Charles Wright. Published by FSG in 2019 in *Oblivion Banjo: The Poetry of Charles Wright*.

James Wright, "The First Days," from *To a Blossoming Pear Tree*, copyright © 1977 by James Wright. Published by FSG in 1977 in *To a Blossoming Pear Tree*.

James Wright, "As I Step over a Puddle at the End of Winter, I Think of an Ancient Chinese Governor," from *The Branch Will Not Break*, copyright © 1963 by James Wright. Published by FSG in 1990 in *Above the River: The Complete Poems*.

Adam Zagajewski, "Russia Comes into Poland," from *Płótno*, copyright © 1990 by Adam Zagajewski. Translation copyright © 1992 by Renata Gorczynski, Benjamin Ivry, and C. K. Williams. Published by FSG in 1992 in *Canvas*.

Adam Zagajewski, "Reading Milosz," from *Eternal Enemies*, copyright © 2008 by Adam Zagajewski. Translation copyright © 2008 by Clare Cavanagh. Published by FSG in 2008 in *Eternal Enemies*.

Adam Zagajewski, "The Calling of St. Matthew," from *Prawdziwe życie*, copyright © 2019 by Adam Zagajewski. Translated by Clare Cavanagh.